TOGETHER WE MARCH

25 PROTEST MOVEMENTS THAT MARCHED INTO HISTORY

LEAH HENDERSON

ILLUSTRATED BY TYLER FEDER

ATHENEUM BOOKS FOR YOUNG READERS

NEW YORK   LONDON   TORONTO   SYDNEY   NEW DELHI

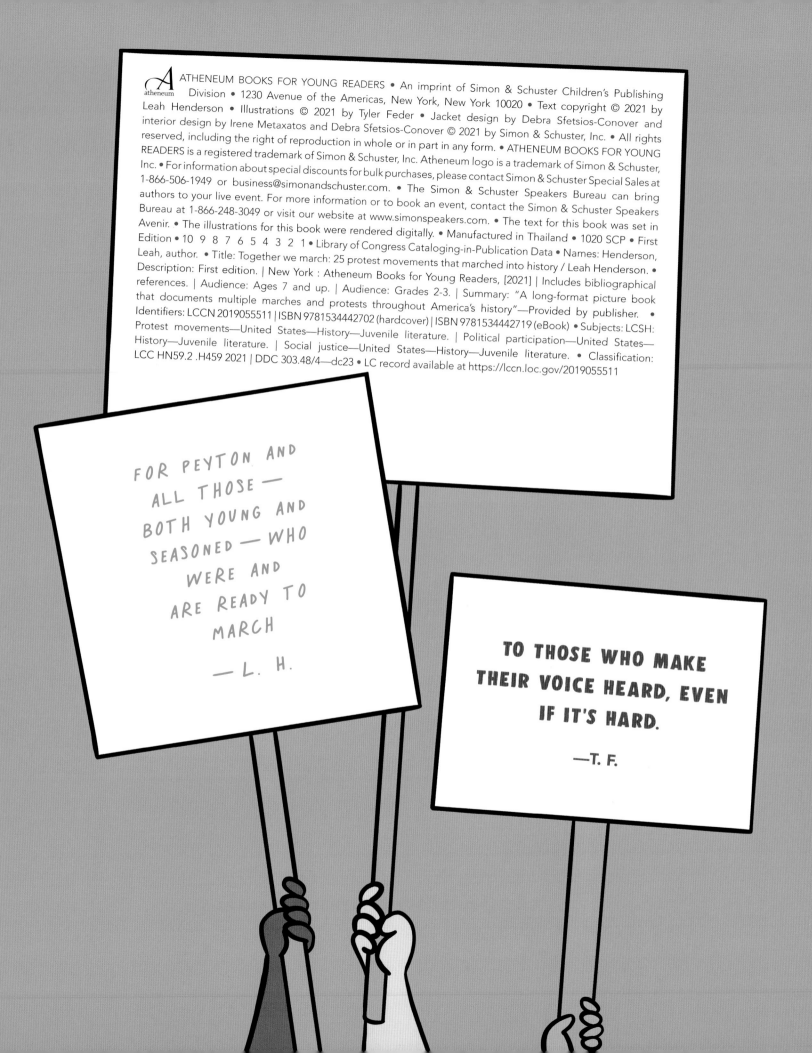

ATHENEUM BOOKS FOR YOUNG READERS • An imprint of Simon & Schuster Children's Publishing Division • 1230 Avenue of the Americas, New York, New York 10020 • Text copyright © 2021 by Leah Henderson • Illustrations © 2021 by Tyler Feder • Jacket design by Debra Sfetsios-Conover and interior design by Irene Metaxatos and Debra Sfetsios-Conover © 2021 by Simon & Schuster, Inc. • All rights reserved, including the right of reproduction in whole or in part in any form. • ATHENEUM BOOKS FOR YOUNG READERS is a registered trademark of Simon & Schuster, Inc. Atheneum logo is a trademark of Simon & Schuster, Inc. • For information about special discounts for bulk purchases, please contact Simon & Schuster Special Sales at 1-866-506-1949 or business@simonandschuster.com. • The Simon & Schuster Speakers Bureau can bring authors to your live event. For more information or to book an event, contact the Simon & Schuster Speakers Bureau at 1-866-248-3049 or visit our website at www.simonspeakers.com. • The text for this book was set in Avenir. • The illustrations for this book were rendered digitally. • Manufactured in Thailand • 1020 SCP • First Edition • 10 9 8 7 6 5 4 3 2 1 • Library of Congress Cataloging-in-Publication Data • Names: Henderson, Leah, author. • Title: Together we march: 25 protest movements that marched into history / Leah Henderson. • Description: First edition. | New York : Atheneum Books for Young Readers, [2021] | Includes bibliographical references. | Audience: Ages 7 and up. | Audience: Grades 2-3. | Summary: "A long-format picture book that documents multiple marches and protests throughout America's history"—Provided by publisher. • Identifiers: LCCN 2019055511 | ISBN 9781534442702 (hardcover) | ISBN 9781534442719 (eBook) • Subjects: LCSH: Protest movements—United States—History—Juvenile literature. | Political participation—United States—History—Juvenile literature. | Social justice—United States—History—Juvenile literature. • Classification: LCC HN59.2 .H459 2021 | DDC 303.48/4—dc23 • LC record available at https://lccn.loc.gov/2019055511

FOR PEYTON AND ALL THOSE— BOTH YOUNG AND SEASONED—WHO WERE AND ARE READY TO MARCH

—L. H.

TO THOSE WHO MAKE THEIR VOICE HEARD, EVEN IF IT'S HARD.

—T. F.

There's something about a march that is very powerful. It's a powerful weapon, a powerful organizing tool, and it has a powerful influence on those who participate. . . . You have a definite starting place and definite goal. You're moving, making progress every step . . . you get a lot of courage. . . . The march picks up its own cadence, its own spirit, its own history.

—Cesar Chavez

INTRODUCTION

IN RECENT YEARS, have you noticed more and more people are taking to the streets to protest? These people are using their feet, their voices, the words on their signs, and the strength in their numbers to combat injustice, oppression, inequality, and discrimination. They protest these wrongs, demand change, and call for further action in their neighborhoods, cities, states, and countries, or even in the world, every day. It may feel like this global surge of speaking out is new, but marching and marchers have a long history.

For decades, marches both great and small have been an invaluable tool to help bring about social change for many marginalized groups. By bringing together people with differing perspectives and experiences under a unified umbrella, the demand that the public, the media, and the government work towards something better for everyone—not just a select few—rings louder and clearer.

By itself, a march can energize a group of people, welcome newcomers to a cause, or give veterans of a fight the power to go on. But marchers also bring awareness of an issue to the public at large, giving strength to a movement, and putting a plan into action. Though a march can be made up of many or simply a few, they all grow from the determination of people, and the collective might of a group. As people march they are no longer just one individual, one voice, one opinion, or one demand.

Even though the overall journey to change may be long, marching can be a powerful and pivotal component in a campaign because this show of numbers can grab the attention of the public in ways other efforts

cannot. By drawing media attention, marches can put faces to the issues and broadcast a clear message that may turn the heads and hearts of those who have remained indifferent. It can also add pressure on people in power as the world's eyes turn to them. Marches are most effective when they are part of a larger movement, but on their own, they have been a rallying cry, a shield in the face of hatred, and the hope needed to remind people they are not alone in what they are facing.

Within these pages you will see when and why people in different eras have marched and continue to march today. You will see how marching brings purpose, support, and optimism to the whole, whether it is at the beginning of a fight, or a continued push.

Within these pages you will also learn of the tremendous sacrifices many have made not just for themselves but for strangers, their families, and their communities. You will discover people who were confronted with imprisonment, threats, or violence, but who did not back down or resort to violence themselves. People who felt that the hope of a better tomorrow was worth the sting of today, even with many miles still left to go.

From these incredible marchers, we learn that even when a fight seems impossible, or a situation or circumstance immovable, marching can be the push needed to tip the scales and create a movement.

You will see how marginalized communities today continue this work in striving for social justice; equal access to things like health care, food, and jobs; and a society where skin color, gender, sexual orientation, ability, or birthplace do not limit these opportunities. You will also see how *everyone*—regardless of who they are and where they are from—can be affected by gun violence, climate change, war, and the suffering of others.

Numbers today may have grown, and technology has certainly changed and advanced our ability to spread our messages, but the core reasons why we march remain the same. In the face of extreme doubt and uncertainty, people of all ages and backgrounds continue to choose to march, believing they can create change and go farther on the heels of those who marched before them.

This book celebrates this rich history and the often-overlooked stories, revered moments, and courageous people who continue to teach us the importance of coming together to march.

**Sometimes it takes extraordinary means to
attract ordinary interest.**

—Mother Jones

TOGETHER WE MARCH TO PROTECT OUR CHILDHOOD

Today, it's hard to imagine children as young as five working alongside men and women on dangerous machines, breathing lint-filled air. However, in textile mills in the early 1900s it was commonplace for kids to spend ten to fourteen hours a day working in these hot rooms instead of going to school. In Pennsylvania, the law prohibited children under the age of twelve from working, but that law was rarely enforced. The wages from millwork were tiny, even with the long hours. Nevertheless, families needed to eat, so every able body contributed.

Factory tasks were often very routine but also dangerous, and mill owners made no effort to make them safer, not even for their youngest employees. So early one June morning in 1903, when the opening bells rang out across Kensington, a neighborhood in northern Philadelphia, Pennsylvania, nearly ninety thousand textile workers, including ten thousand children, did not show up for work. Instead they banded together to strike for better wages, shorter hours, and safer working conditions. Despite this, the mill owners did not fold. They simply waited for their poor, malnourished workers to give up.

Not everyone ignored the workers, though. Mary "Mother" Harris Jones, an Irish immigrant and prominent labor and community organizer, heard them loud and clear. At almost seventy, she was known to many as "the most dangerous woman in America" because she spoke her mind and was not afraid to act.

As soon as she saw the stooped frames, bent knees, and sickly faces of the child strikers, she knew they needed more than just a shorter work week—they needed protection under the law. However, since the mill owners owned stock in the newspapers, the papers never covered these abuses, and the general public did not seem to know or care about the plight of the mill children.

But Mother Jones had a mind to change that! On July 7, 1903, she and some say almost two hundred children—known as her "industrial army"—along with about one hundred adults set out from Kensington led by a fife and drum. The children carried banners reading, WE WANT TO GO TO SCHOOL and WE ONLY ASK FOR JUSTICE. Their plan was to march over ninety miles to New York City to gain the public's attention.

Mother Jones held rallies and gave speeches in the towns they marched through. She lifted the youngest children up high, showing their hollowed chests, deformed shoulders, and mangled fingers. Soon pastors and universities all over the country were talking about Mother Jones and the mill children. People were finally listening.

This gave Mother Jones another idea. Wouldn't more people hear them if they marched their concerns right to the president? Their final destination quickly changed to Oyster Bay, New York, which was another thirty-five miles away and where President Theodore Roosevelt vacationed with his family.

Day after day, carrying knapsacks and banners, the young marchers faced heat, rain, mosquitoes, and other hardships. Even though their bodies were frail and overworked, they were eager to do their part. Farmers gave them fruit and vegetables, and other supporters provided donations, clothes, and shelter to help them.

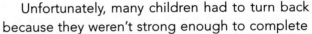

Unfortunately, many children had to turn back because they weren't strong enough to complete the journey. Undaunted, Mother Jones and three determined young crusaders journeyed to the president, arriving on the twenty-second day of their march. Though the president refused to see them, the rest of the country did not. Their march brought much-needed attention to the cruelty of child labor practices and the effect they had on these children, as thousands came to hear Mother Jones and the children at each stop. And this attention helped lead to the creation of the National Child Labor Committee one year later. Progress was slow, but after twelve years, in 1915, Pennsylvania finally passed a law prohibiting children under the age of fourteen from working. A year after that, the federal government created its first child labor law, which would start to protect children across the country.

The march of the mill children was one of the first juvenile marches in US history. Alone, their voices might have been small; however, together, they were mighty, showing that kids just like you can make a difference.

MUD MARCH

Rise up, women, for the fight is hard and long;
Rise up in thousands singing loud a battle song.
Right is might, and in strength we shall be strong,
And the cause goes marching on.
—"Rise Up Women!" song by Theodora Mills

TOGETHER WE MARCH FOR A WOMAN'S RIGHT TO VOTE

While the mill children of Pennsylvania were picking up their signs, women in Great Britain were campaigning for a woman's right to vote. They thought it only fair that since they were expected to follow the laws, they should get a say in who was passing them.

However, not everyone agreed on how to achieve this goal. Some believed in more reserved, law-abiding approaches, like leaflets, petitions, and public meetings. Others had grown tired of being nice and felt more active protest was needed. A suffrage organization called the Women's Social and Political Union (WSPU) became known for standing on chairs, disrupting government meetings, and being willing to break the law. Soon members found themselves in jail for assaulting police or for refusing to pay fines. Although the public often disapproved, for some it was also fascinating to see women employing these methods.

Other groups, including the leading suffrage organization, the National Union of Women's Suffrage Societies (NUWSS), disagreed with the WSPU's tactics. Still, their leader, Millicent Fawcett, noticed something very crucial: the WSPU garnered press attention in a way her group did not. She realized it was the perfect time to embrace the determination of the "suffragettes"—a term used for the more extreme campaigners— and find a way to continue the momentum they'd started, through more peaceful means.

Millicent and her female "suffragists" decided they'd hold a public procession in the streets at the next opening session of Parliament. Although this may not seem controversial or daring today, in the early 1900s the idea of women parading in the street was almost scandalous! However, after many telegrams, letters, some telephone calls, and two newspaper advertisements, hundreds of women, even noblewomen, agreed to attend. For some suffragists, this meant risking public shaming, their employment, and friendships. But their determination was greater than the risk, and they were ready to show the government and public by their numbers how committed they were to getting the vote.

On the day of the march, the weather was cold and dreary, so the organizers weren't certain who might attend. But on that rainy, fog-filled Saturday, women

from all over Britain, wealthy and aristocratic ladies, scholars in university caps and gowns, high school headmistresses, artists, textile workers, typists, nurses, seamstresses, and teachers, all showed up to march. More than forty organizations and three thousand soaking-wet women in silk and velvet, with sashes and banners, sloshed through the muddy streets of London.

Onlookers pressed in, not believing the sight. Some laughed or pointed, but many were simply astonished that white women from all classes had put aside their differences and were marching side by side, their long skirts sweeping across the mud. The suffragists marched, heads held high, about a mile and a half, from Hyde Park Corner to Exeter Hall, near Trafalgar Square. They carried signs and embroidered organization banners, stating GENTLE, BUT RESOLUTE and BE RIGHT AND PERSIST. The procession of women, three female bands, and a line of motorcars, wagons, hansoms, and carriages stretched for half a mile.

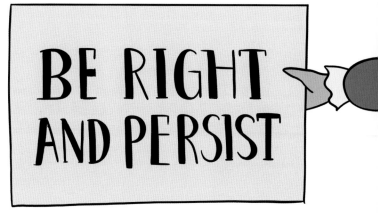

By today's measure, these numbers may appear small, but in 1907 the Mud March was one of the largest marches ever held. It was also the first led by women for the rights of women. By marching, they'd not only gained the attention of London, but also the world. Newspapers in the US, Canada, and Australia carried their story. In Britain they were even front-page news!

Although no immediate action was taken in Parliament, the momentum and publicity encouraged the NUWSS to continue holding marches. By 1911, their demonstrations had swelled from three thousand to forty thousand women. Due in large part to the muddy marchers, women over age thirty with British university degrees and property gained the right to vote in 1918, and full rights were granted to all women over age twenty-one in 1928.

By pushing themselves to defy expectations of a woman's role for all the world to see, these suffragists challenged the ideas and justifications men in power used to keep the vote away from them. There was still a long way to go for full equality, but with their voices and their feet, women marching together let those who opposed them know that they belonged everywhere men did—including the voting booth!

BE RIGHT AND PERSIST

SILENT PROTEST PARADE

New York, New York
July 28, 1917

We live in spite of death shadowing us and ours. We prosper in the face of the most unwarranted and illegal oppression.

—NAACP flyer for the march

TOGETHER WE MARCH TO BE TREATED AS EQUAL CITIZENS

At a time when women were demanding voting rights, Black Americans were also demanding the vote and equal protection under the law. It had been more than fifty years since the end of the Civil War and their emancipation from slavery; however, Black citizens were far from free or equal. In the South, Jim Crow laws segregated access to schools, pools, elevators, hospitals, and more, by designating many as "whites only." Also, southern Black citizens often faced bleak economic opportunities, and many were denied voting rights through poll taxes they couldn't afford, literacy tests they weren't meant to pass, and other forms of racial oppression. And discrimination wasn't just by law. Black Americans faced the constant threat of violence as well.

In the first five months of 1916 alone, thirty-one Black Americans were publicly killed by mobs, but the white perpetrators of the lynchings were never charged. Frustrated and angered by these countless acts of violence, as well as by segregation laws and poor job prospects, hundreds of thousands of Black citizens fled the South in what became known as the Great Migration. They hoped for a safer and more prosperous future in the North, where factories were growing to meet the demands of the First World War. However, due in part to limited housing and jobs, not all northern cities were welcoming, and Black Americans faced violence there, too.

When a factory owner in East St. Louis, Illinois, hired newly arrived southern Black workers as strikebreakers, displacing local white workers, and a white officer was killed during racial tensions, white mobs set fires to houses in Black neighborhoods. They intentionally cut water supplies, shot or stoned Black people trying to flee the burning buildings, and ultimately burned ten blocks of homes. The rioting went on throughout the night as the National Guard and the mayor did little to help. As many as two hundred Black citizens were killed, including the young and disabled, and six thousand were left homeless.

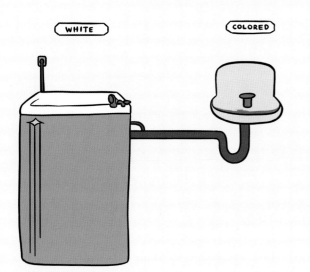

The executive committee of the Harlem, New York City, branch of the newly formed National Association for the Advancement of Colored People (NAACP) quickly came together after the terrible incident to figure out a response. Many wanted to hold an urgent meeting, but prominent member and noted civil rights activist James Weldon Johnson suggested a silent parade: no colorful clothing, chanting, or singing; simply determined Black souls marching as one in silence against injustice. Silence would provoke a striking scene, but also speak to the fact that for far too long, the government and the public had been silent on the violence faced by Black citizens. Through a big showing of their own silence and dignity, marchers hoped to draw attention and force the government to confront the issues.

More than ten thousand Black residents of the greater New York area heard the call. So, at 1:00 p.m. on a hot July day in 1917, Johnson strode out in front of the crowd with other Black leaders, including NAACP founding member and scholar W. E. B. DuBois and Rev. Dr. H. C. Bishop, the president of the parade. Women and children all in white marched hand in hand, while men marched behind in dark suits and military uniforms. While Boy Scouts distributed leaflets to inform onlookers about the discrimination, segregation, and lynching of Black Americans, muffled drums were the only sounds heard.

During the two-mile-long march from Fifth Avenue, New York's wealthiest street, to Madison Square, protesters let their banners and posters tell the story of why they marched. Never had such a sight been seen in New York, or in all the world. When certain banners passed onlookers, applause rang out in agreement from both white and brown hands. After the march, a petition was sent to the White House urging President Wilson to support anti-lynching legislation.

Even though marchers were unified in their belief, sadly the rest of the country did not unite behind the cause. Instead of heeding their call for protections under the law, President Wilson went against his campaign promises to support Black Americans and further segregated the federal government. However, while the Silent Protest Parade didn't achieve its ultimate goal, the march was the beginning of mass nonviolent protest marches against racial violence that would continue through the Civil Rights era and beyond.

GIVE US A CHANCE TO LIVE

SO TREAT US SO WE MAY LOVE OUR COUNTRY

SALT MARCH

I want world sympathy in this battle of right against might.

—Mahatma Gandhi

TOGETHER WE MARCH FOR INDEPENDENCE

While Black Americans were publicly demanding protection as equal citizens, the people of India were striving to be independent and self-governing after almost two hundred years under British colonial control. English ships had initially sailed to India to partake in trade, but the British Crown soon found heavily taxing Indian citizens to be even more lucrative.

By 1928, the Indian National Congress (INC), a political party started by the people of India yearning for independence, had had enough. They created a declaration of independence that they formally approved the next year, but the British government ignored it. At that time, Indians had already been engaging in several nonviolent protests and boycotts that challenged unjust British laws. However, one of the nationalist movement's leaders, the lawyer and well-known social activist Mohandas "Mahatma" Gandhi, understood stronger, more visible action needed to be taken.

MAHATMA GANDHI

He proposed a nonviolent protest challenging the Salt Act of 1882. Although salt taxes had been abolished in Britain in 1825, the Salt Act of 1882 kept Indians from collecting and selling salt from the sea as they had always done. Instead, they had to buy it from government shops where it was heavily taxed. Many in the INC initially disagreed with this campaign, not understanding how salt could make an impact. They were wrong.

Disobeying the Salt Act was a perfect and relatable nonviolent way to rally the whole public to challenge the overall system of unjust rule. Salt was something everyone used, so the tax affected them all. Plans were soon underway, and on March 12, 1930, the sixty-one-year-old Gandhi and seventy-nine of his followers set out from his ashram, or spiritual home, near Ahmedabad, India, to begin the 240-mile journey to a small seaside village, far away on the Arabian Sea. Each day the protesters marched ten to twelve miles, and newspapers across the globe documented their journey. Like the marchers who came before him, Gandhi knew the media attention would raise global awareness of the injustices they faced under British rule and garner public support and sympathy needed for the larger cause of Indian independence.

Gandhi defies Britain; Makes Salt in India

People lined roadsides and watched from open windows, tree branches, and anywhere else they might get a glimpse of the marchers. At each stop, Gandhi spoke out against British rule and the salt tax and called for people to protest in whatever way they could beyond this one march—boycotting, demonstrating, or picketing. Sometimes crowds grew larger than twenty thousand, but police did not take action. The government feared a backlash and did not want to make Gandhi a martyr in front of the world.

The march took twenty-four days and grew with each step. By the time they reached the coastal village of Dandi, the eighty marchers had grown to thousands, and journalists were on hand to witness it. Days before, police had ground the salt crust along the seashore into the wet sand to make it hard for Gandhi and his followers to collect it. But this did not stop him. He did not need pounds of salt to defy the government. He only needed a few grains. Reaching down, he scooped up a handful of salt-rich sand and said, "With this, I am shaking the foundations of the British empire." Gandhi could easily have taken a car straight to the seashore, but he knew the importance of each step of the march that had brought them there.

Through his small act of defiance and civil disobedience, he started a movement. Millions followed his lead in breaking the law by making, selling, and illegally buying salt to defy British rule. Although the salt protest did not bring an end to the salt tax, marching to collect a few grains of salt highlighted a foreign power's oppressive hand and galvanized a nation, soon bringing Britain and India to the negotiating table as equals. Once they had begun, the people of India refused to stop fighting the injustice of British rule until India gained its independence seventeen years later.

BULGARIAN JEWS MARCH

Sofia, Bulgaria
May 24, 1943

You know what you have to do. Let the trains leave empty, we shall stay here, we shall not go to the slaughter.

—Rabbi Asher Hananel, Sofia's de facto chief rabbi

TOGETHER WE MARCH BECAUSE IT IS THE ONLY WAY

While the people of India continued their struggle for independence, Bulgaria's Jewish population was fighting to survive. For hundreds of years, Bulgarian Jews and Christians had lived together as equals. They respected each other's religious beliefs and on occasion participated in each other's religious activities. They shopped at each other's businesses, attended the same parties, spoke the same language, and shared meals. For five hundred years, they'd suffered, starved, and struggled together under Turkish rule, and in World War I, they fought side by side. The Bulgarian constitution and many of its citizens saw all people as equal regardless of religion or ethnicity.

Then, in the 1930s when Adolf Hitler and his Nazi Party rose to power in Germany, life and ideals across much of Europe shifted. King Boris III of Bulgaria agreed to become an ally of Adolf Hitler and Nazi Germany, and some Bulgarian people began to adopt the Nazi hatred against Jews as well. Nazi youth groups began to form, and Bulgaria soon introduced anti-Jewish laws, which saw Jewish people as noncitizens and enemies of the state, stripping them of many rights both personally and professionally.

Although the Bulgarian government had turned on its Jewish population, many of the country's non-Jewish citizens had not. Hundreds of open letters, telegrams, and petitions poured into the capital city of Sofia. People from every walk of life opposed this treatment of their Jewish neighbors and friends and demanded these laws be changed.

But even in the face of protests and local support, oppression of the Jewish population increased. Hitler and pro-Nazi Bulgarian leaders wanted all Jews deported from Bulgarian territories, so in March of 1943 over eleven thousand Jews from Bulgarian-controlled territories were sent to Nazi-run death camps in Poland with very little protest. However, when word spread that the same fate awaited Jewish families, friends, and neighbors in the "old lands," Bulgaria itself, people across the country finally moved to act.

On May 24, 1943, a national holiday of Bulgarian alphabet, knowledge, and culture, Metropolitan Stefan of the Bulgarian Orthodox Church gave a few harsh words at the end of his speech in front of many government officials and non-Jewish citizens in Sofia saying the celebration was "flawed" because the Jewish students were no longer permitted to be a part of the festivities. On that day instead, many in the Jewish population were meeting in a small synagogue in a Jewish neighborhood to pray and discuss their fate. Hundreds more surrounded the synagogue as well. With the news of their almost certain deportation, there began rumblings about public protest, and after some hesitation, the Jewish public gathered there agreed to march.

Hundreds of Jews from Sofia and some non-Jewish supporters were ready to march to the palace of the king to demand he protect the Jewish population because they were Bulgarian citizens. Wearing their government-mandated yellow stars of David, the Jewish citizens, marching behind a national flag, were bold in their act of defiance against Hitler and the pro-Nazi government of Bulgaria. With each step, Bulgarian Jews showed they were willing to fight for their survival and would not go quietly. Jewish men, women, and children marched from the synagogue a number of blocks before they were confronted by police armed with rifles, submachine guns, and whips. Many Jews were beaten and hundreds were arrested, though some were able to hide in sympathizers' homes, churches, and even in a non-Jewish bakery. The march did not make it far, but it showed Jewish resilience and the bonds of neighbors and friends as non-Jews rallied alongside them. In no other country during the war did such a protest happen.

Although the Jewish population of Sofia and most other large cities and southern towns was transported to labor camps and transportation centers in the north, no trains ever reached Poland. In fact, they never left Bulgaria. King Boris III had changed his mind. Due in large part to Christian and Jewish leaders and the citizens of Bulgaria demanding protection of all citizens, 48,000 Jews from Bulgaria were saved during the Holocaust.

Though the war would not end for two more years, and many more Jewish people were killed throughout Europe, this march was an important lesson that even those with little power can make heroic things happen by standing up for one another.

WOMEN STRIKE FOR PEACE

Nationwide, United States
November 1, 1961

The sit-in strikers have reminded us, as the suffragettes did long ago, of the tremendous power for good in each single person.

—Patricia Kempler, a WSP march organizer in Los Angeles

TOGETHER WE MARCH TO SAVE THE HUMAN RACE

During World War II, while the Jewish community of Sofia marched against orders for their forced removal, America and the Soviet Union, which included Russia and fourteen other surrounding countries, fought as allies against Hitler and the Nazis. However, these two countries did not share the same political and economic views. While the United States is a democracy and values individual freedom, the Soviet Union was communist and believed in shared ownership by government and community. After the defeat of Germany and its allies, as Europe debated how to rebuild, Americans and Soviets soon began to think that the other was planning to destroy their political system and threaten their way of life.

Each nation believed that in order to contain the other's might, it needed increased military and nuclear capability. Soon the two superpowers were in an "arms race" to build the most advanced nuclear weapons. And to do so, they needed to test them. Although the US government told Americans that aboveground nuclear testing was safe, a number of scientists and physicists around the world disagreed. Studies showed that after an explosion, the fallout—particles of harmful radioactive dust—could be carried on the wind, or fall to the ground and be consumed by grazing animals, especially cows. Their milk would then affect humans who drank it, even causing radioactive compounds to grow in children's bones.

DAGMAR WILSON

WOMEN STRIKE FOR PEACE

When children's book illustrator Dagmar Wilson and six friends discussed these issues in her Washington, DC, home in 1961, little did they know it would be the start of a movement. They didn't consider themselves activists, but they realized if they could spread the reports of the effects of contaminated milk on children, mothers and other women especially would rally to protest nuclear testing on their behalf. And so "Women Strike for Peace" was formed.

Their focus was to highlight dangers of aboveground testing, to demand "Pure Milk Not Poison," and to call for a ban

from both the US and Soviet powers on nuclear weapons testing. They planned a large rally and march to the White House, but also urged individuals in communities across the country to create their own protest activities under the umbrella of the larger organization. Within six weeks, through word of mouth and Christmas card address lists, the group had notified women across the country about their goals for the nationwide protest.

On November 1, 1961, more than twelve thousand women in sixty cities throughout America took part in the strike. Female college students, teenagers, mothers, widows, university professors, teachers, and grandmothers marched together to local government buildings. Some held babies or pushed strollers and many carried signs. Dagmar Wilson's group, along with more than a thousand others, even marched to the White House and the Soviet Embassy in DC. There they delivered letters to First Lady Jacqueline Kennedy and to the Soviet Union's First Lady, Nina Khrushchev, urging them to speak with their husbands to stop this harmful testing. Women marchers demanded that the country "End the Arms Race, Not the Human Race."

Some of them were met by applause, others with blank stares. While some officials agreed to carry their message of peace to the president, others told them to redirect their anger to the Soviets or refused to give them an audience at all. Regardless, the women continued to march and gained nationwide attention. Many newspapers marveled at their ability to come together from all different backgrounds in such force in just six weeks for this protest. It was a message to everyone that one person reaching out to even just a few people, like Dagmar Wilson did, can make a difference.

In part because of their voices and the attention paid to their cause by the media and political groups, two years later the Soviet Union and the United States signed the 1963 Nuclear Test Ban Treaty, which banned nuclear weapons tests in the air, in outer space, and underwater. While nuclear weapons have not yet been eliminated, this was an important step toward making the world safer.

These women are a reminder that even if you do not consider yourself an activist, taking even a small action can start a whole movement!

CHILDREN'S MARCH
(THE CHILDREN'S CRUSADE)

Birmingham, Alabama
May 2–7, 1963

Don't worry about your children, they're gonna be all right. Don't hold them back if they want to go to jail. For they are doing a job for all of America and for all mankind.

—Rev. Dr. Martin Luther King Jr.

TOGETHER WE MARCH FOR AN END TO "SEPARATE BUT EQUAL"

Much like the newly engaged activism of members of "Women Strike for Peace," Black youth in the south understood they were needed. Action was just as necessary as it had been during the Silent Protest Parade in the 1920s and beyond. In the 1940s, '50s, and '60s Black demonstrators continued to demand protection and equal rights under the law because they did not truly garner the same rights as white citizens anywhere in the US, especially not in the South.

Injustices were happening all over the country, but nowhere more so than in Birmingham, Alabama. There had been more bombings of Black homes and churches in Birmingham than in any other American city. Black workers were paid far less than their white counterparts, and "whites only" and "colored only" signs hung throughout the city's downtown. Local Black leaders, led by Rev. Fred Shuttlesworth, made countless attempts to meet with Birmingham's white leadership to negotiate changes on behalf of the Black community, but they were ignored. They needed direct action. So on April 3, 1963, they boycotted local businesses, had sit-ins at white lunch counters and libraries, took part in kneel-ins at white churches to gauge the churches' openness for desegregated worship, and held mass meetings to discuss further strategies.

White city officials fought back. They went to the courts to legally stop protesters. However, Black citizens kept protesting, and soon thousands were jailed. As more people were arrested and concern grew among them about losing their jobs or being evicted from their homes if they protested, it was proposed that children could lead the campaign. At first, not many agreed. Protesting could be dangerous. But adults were not the only ones who wanted change. Young people were tired of department stores and libraries being closed to them. They were tired of looking through fences at playgrounds and ball fields they couldn't use and amusement park rides they couldn't ride. Like their parents, they wanted to fight, and marching was something they could do.

By word of mouth the plan spread and thousands of young students—some as young as six or seven years old—agreed to march on May 2, 1963, a day they called "D-Day" (Demonstration Day). When the signal was given, these kids climbed out of schoolhouse windows and rushed through doors to get out and march. Some came from as far as eighteen miles away.

In groups of fifty, they left the 16th Street Baptist Church and headed toward downtown Birmingham. After only a few blocks, local white authorities arrested them for parading without a permit. But as soon as they did, fifty more students marched from the church. By day's end, more than eight hundred students had been carried to jail in school buses and police wagons. By the second day, Double D-Day, jails and holding facilities were full almost to bursting and Black classrooms were nearly empty. Nevertheless, the students kept on coming. In frustration and hatred for the parading children and what they stood for, Public Safety Commissioner Eugene "Bull" Conner roared at fire departments to spray the peaceful young marchers with high-powered water hoses. But still more students came. Soon, additional force was ordered, and policemen clubbed non-violent marchers with batons, while attack dogs pulled at their bodies and clothes.

And yet the young people still kept coming.

The nightly news broadcast the alarming scenes into living rooms across the country. Newspapers splashed the troubling stories on their pages. The world saw what happened to Black children in Birmingham when they asked for equality. So, as the world watched, moved by the children's courage and determination and not wanting any more harm to come to them, pressure built and negotiations began from as high as the White House. Just as people had upon seeing the mill children with Mother Jones, Americans could no longer ignore the students' demand for fair treatment.

By May 10, an agreement had been reached. "White" and "Colored" signs would come down, lunch counters and fitting rooms would become open to all, and every jailed protester would be released. Over three thousand young people in Birmingham fearlessly marching together would not soon be forgotten. There was still a long way to go, but their brave efforts gave much-needed momentum to the nationwide call for racial equality and showed us the power to take a stand is possible within even the youngest of us.

Jim Crow MUST GO

POLICE

MARCH ON WASHINGTON FOR JOBS AND FREEDOM

We must say: "Wake up, America! Wake up!" For we cannot stop, and we will not and cannot be patient.

—John Lewis

TOGETHER WE MARCH FOR OPPORTUNITY

Images of Black children, marching two by two, being attacked on the streets of Birmingham, Alabama, were still fresh in people's minds in 1963. Not just in America, but all over the world. People realized that American Black people had no legal means to fight discrimination. The law did not protect them, so they had no choice but to take their grievances to the streets, where racial protests were happening in cities all over the country.

President Kennedy was sickened by what he saw in the South, troubled by the discontent in the North, and unsettled by how America was viewed abroad. He believed, despite disagreement from advisors, that he needed to submit a strong civil rights bill. But for the bill to become law, it would need to be passed by Congress. Black Americans knew pressure needed to be put on a largely undecided Congress to vote in favor of the bill that would finally offer them federal protection for equal access to public facilities, public education, and voting rights. To do this, they would have to continue the momentum they had ignited and bring their issues to Washington—the seat of power.

While Dr. King and the Southern Christian Leadership Conference started planning a march for freedom, A. Philip Randolph, a labor organizer and prominent civil rights activist, had long been hoping to create a similar protest in Washington, but for job opportunities. Understanding there was strength in numbers, King and Randolph came together, and the March on Washington for Jobs and Freedom was born. At first, President Kennedy feared the march was ill-timed and could harm the outcome of the bill

LIVE & WORK TOGETHER

WE DEMAND VOTING RIGHTS NOW!

JIM CROW MUST GO!

WE MARCH FOR FIRST CLASS CITIZENSHIP NOW!

I'M SKATING TO WASHINGTON DC FOR CIVIL RIGHTS AND THE NAACP

WE DEMAND EQUAL RIGHTS NOW

before Congress if a disturbance broke out. But King and Randolph disagreed, reassuring the president that it would be an orderly and respectful affair. Leaders of the main civil rights groups of the time gathered to help sponsor the march, and a short time later, groups outside the Black community, like the United Auto Workers and the American Jewish Congress, joined them. The organizers planned for 100,000 people to attend, but on the day of the march, 250,000 arrived! Hardly a speck of grass could be seen. The crowd was made up of about 190,000 Black demonstrators and 60,000 allies. Early in the day, people arrived at the Washington Monument from all over—one had even traveled on roller skates all the way from Chicago, Illinois! People of different backgrounds held hands and locked arms, singing. At that time, it was the largest turnout Washington had ever seen.

Grasping arms and holding signs demanding voting rights, civil rights, and freedom, marchers moved down Constitution Avenue almost propelled by the energy and force of the crowd. People marched about nine blocks together showing they understood that if injustice happened to even one person, injustice was happening to everyone. When the protesters reached the Lincoln Memorial, the crowd was thick, fanning themselves in the 83-degree heat. Some sat high in nearby trees, eager to see the main ceremony. Celebrities, ministers, teachers, janitors, Christians, and Jews stood shoulder to shoulder, speaking with their sheer numbers as Dr. King spoke about his now famous dream.

The March on Washington wasn't just about demanding that legislation get passed in Congress for Black jobs and freedom, it was also about hope and giving encouragement to those frustrated by the slow process of change. It said, don't give up, don't turn back, and don't let anger overtake the will to keep marching. Congress passing the bill would be important, yes, but what was equally as important was the renewed energy and strength Black Americans and others received that day. Twenty million Black citizens and others across the country heard the message that they couldn't rest until everyone was truly free.

They kept fighting for their cause, and less than one year later, the Civil Rights Act of 1964—which ended legal racial segregation and made discrimination unlawful—was signed, and the Voting Rights Act of 1965 followed shortly after. While racism and discrimination did not disappear from the United States, they did become illegal after decades of people marching, showing that no matter how slow, real change is possible when we continue to come together.

FREE SPEECH MOVEMENT AND MARCH

Berkeley, California
November 20, 1964

There's a time when the operation of the machine becomes so odious, makes you so sick at heart that you can't take part! . . . And you've got to put your bodies upon the gears and upon the wheels, upon the levers, upon all the apparatus—and you've got to make it stop!

—Mario Savio, member of Berkeley Free Speech Movement

TOGETHER WE MARCH FOR THE FREEDOM TO SPEAK OUR MINDS

When Dr. King said that 1963 was "not an end, but a beginning," for many listening it was a shift from sitting on the sidelines to stepping up and becoming a voice in the demand for change.

By then, students were already on the front lines of protest movements, and they were spreading the word to friends on college campuses across the country, such as at the University of California at Berkeley. For some of the predominantly white UC Berkeley students who found themselves in handcuffs right alongside Black protesters, it was their first contact with the injustices minority groups in America had been facing for decades. Instead of turning away though, they became even more involved.

At Berkeley, a large part of spreading the word about these movements happened on a tiny strip of brick walkway on the edge of the university grounds. By manning tables, handing out leaflets, collecting donations, and recruiting members for politically driven organizations and causes, students were active in getting the word out about a number of issues there. So when the university informed them this was no longer allowed because it encouraged unlawful activity by students that often led to arrests, students were outraged. The brick walkway was the best place to reach students, as everyone passed it on the way to and from classes, and banning their presence there would essentially cut off much civil rights protest discussion and support. Angered, students believed the university was taking away their constitutional right to free speech, so when the administration refused to reconsider, students realized they'd have to apply the methods they'd learned in civil rights protests to solve this problem.

Soon they were defying the rules, continuing to set up their tables on the walkway, but also in front of the administration building, something they'd never done before. What started as small acts of civil disobedience soon ballooned and garnered the attention of thousands of Berkeley students. They felt the university had overstepped, not only by policing what students advocated for, but by taking disciplinary action against students engaged in unlawful activity off campus grounds as well. This was much more than a campus issue.

For the next few months the UC Berkeley campus became home to the Free Speech Movement. Class attendance numbers were low, and the local police often responded to rallies and sit-ins. Soon media began covering the protests, carrying the campaign for free speech to cities, towns, and college campuses around the world.

After much fruitless back and forth with committees and school administration, student leaders of the Free Speech Movement, such as Mario Salvo and Arthur Goldberg, announced a rally and silent march. They wanted the march to bring together everyone in the university community who believed in the students' right to free speech. The march wasn't about global attention, or even disruption; it was about uniting people who might not share one another's opinions, but who did share the belief that they had the right to express them. Movement leaders called for students to get permissions from professors to participate, and encouraged faculty to be monitors. Students, teaching assistants, faculty, and others in the community were being asked to take a side.

And on November 20, they did. Three thousand people moved as one from the student union plaza to University Hall, where the administration's board of regents was holding a meeting about how to handle the Free Speech Movement they believed had disrupted the campus for far too many months. Although the march did not change much policy that day, it did motivate the students to keep demonstrating and to stand together for a common belief.

After another few months of protest, and a new chancellor's arrival, the university agreed to open select campus areas to students for social action. However, unlawful off-campus acts generated by on-campus activity would still be disciplined. It wasn't everything the student leaders wanted, and free speech remains a hotly debated topic in schools, but the example the students of UC Berkeley set would help inform future protest movements on campuses across the country that still occur today. Above all, these students' protest helped protect all people's right to protest and speak up for what they believed in.

DELANO TO SACRAMENTO MARCH

Delano, California, to Sacramento, California
March 17–April 10, 1966

I feel we have the same rights as any of them. Because in that Constitution, it said that everybody has equal rights and justice. You've got to make that come about. They are not going to give it to you.

—Larry Itliong

TOGETHER WE MARCH FOR OUR RIGHT TO ORGANIZE

"Welga!" shouted the Filipino farm workers, ready to strike. By September of 1965, they were no strangers to demanding a fairer wage. In the early 1900s, they'd come to California to become migrant workers. Most took the journey alone, believing America would be a land of opportunity. However, like other marginalized groups, they soon found America's freedoms were not entirely for everyone.

Laws barred them from citizenship, voting, owning property, starting a business, and interracial marriage. This left many of the Filipino men poor and single. Farming was hard work for very little pay; without families to support them when they could no longer work, older men, known as "manongs," would need to find another way to provide for themselves.

At the start of the 1965 grape-picking season, these workers went on strike demanding a pay increase in Coachella Valley, California. Growers agreed and increased wages from $1.25 to $1.40 per hour, which was better, though still well below a living wage. But a few months later, when workers asked growers in Delano, California, for a similar raise, the Delano growers refused. These growers had more power, influence, and the backing of the police and local officials.

The manongs, led by labor organizer Larry Itliong and the predominately Filipino Agricultural Workers Organization Committee (AWOC), decided to strike again. More than fifteen hundred Filipino workers picketed, but growers fought back through intimidation and violence, and eventually hired Mexican workers to take the strikers' places.

Filipino labor organizers knew they were losing ground. They approached Cesar Chavez and Dolores Huerta—leaders of the

SACRAMENTO

DELANO

mainly Mexican-American National Farm Workers Association (NFWA)—about joining their efforts. At first there was hesitation, but both communities wanted the same things—better wages, contracts, and overtime along with health care, restrooms, safer tools, more food, and adequate shelter. So Mexican workers voted and agreed, it was time to join the strike!

But when the picket line grew longer, growers grew tougher. They kicked laborers out of camps they'd lived in for years; shut off water, lights, and gas so workers couldn't cook or bathe; and hired armed guards to intimidate strikers. So, in order for the strike to succeed, it needed to go beyond the reach of Delano, where growers had the power to quash it, to the public. Strikers called for a mass boycott of table grapes. Students flocked to Delano to join the picket lines, but the harassment and danger worsened.

Protest organizers determined that a march to Sacramento, the state capital, was the next best step. It would draw media attention, public support, and would also help put distance between strikers and the violence. Six months after the start of the strike, seventy-five farm workers began the three-hundred-mile march, walking single file along the roadway with the American, Mexican, and Philippine flags out in front. Starting on March 17, 1966, they marched through the "valley of their labor," fifty-three towns in all. They depended on the generosity of strangers, churches, and civic organizations to provide food, water, and shelter. Like the March of the Mill Children and the Salt March, in each town they stopped to make speeches, educating the public about their cause, and support quickly grew. At the end of the twenty-five-day journey, ten thousand had joined the original seventy-five in *la causa*. Television cameras and journalists were there to document it all.

Marching was not the end of the fight, but it helped to spark renewed energy so farm workers could continue their tireless strike and boycott, and it provided the visibility they needed. Soon shoppers, grocery stores, and community markets refused to buy or sell California grapes. It took five years, but finally farm workers received their first contract from grape growers. In the process, their merged union, the United Farm Workers of America (UFW), was also officially recognized and protected. And soon after, UFW members and volunteers built a government-supported housing complex for the retired manongs. Today, unions still struggle for recognition and to protect workers' rights, just like these workers did so many years ago. But their years of tireless work in the fields and on the picket lines serve as an example of how much more we can accomplish when we all march together.

"THE MARCH AGAINST DEATH" MORATORIUM TO END THE WAR IN VIETNAM

Washington, DC
November 13–15, 1969

Nothing is more precious than independence and liberty.

—Ho Chi Minh

TOGETHER WE MARCH TO CALL AN END TO WAR

DEMOCRATIC REPUBLIC OF VIETNAM

STATE OF VIETNAM

Thousands of miles from where the California farm workers were striking, the people of Vietnam were engaged in a struggle for independence, not unlike that of India in the early 1900s. The Vietnamese had been under French rule since the mid-nineteenth century, and although many Americans understood their desire to govern themselves, with the Cold War raging, the prospect of an independent Vietnam falling under control of Communist China or Russia seemed a far greater concern.

America's involvement in the ongoing conflict was gradual. France eventually withdrew after years of fighting, but the American government still wanted to ensure the new independent Vietnam would be a democratic nation. Vietnam soon split in two. The north received aid from communist China and Russia, while the United States forged an alliance with South Vietnam. But leaders in both regions still wanted an independent and unified country. They just couldn't agree on how that would look.

Soon US combat troops entered a war that had already cost US taxpayers millions of dollars and all too soon would also cost countless young lives, especially those of the poor, the working class, and minorities. For the first time, horrors of war were broadcast on every television, and much like the images of Black children in Birmingham being blasted by water hoses, seeing the graphic images of American bombings destroying homes, villages, crops, and lives caused many Americans to question what the US was truly fighting for. Opposition to the war had already been increasing on college campuses across the country for several years, but as more Americans lost their lives, support for the war continued to diminish. People of all ages and backgrounds took to the streets in varying forms of protest.

NOT ONE MORE DEAD!

Then, during the weekend of November 15, 1969, they came together. Some estimates say half a million people descended on Washington, DC, to participate in the Moratorium to End the War in Vietnam. The moratorium—a pause or interruption in a person's daily activities—was hosted by one hundred organizations that comprised the National Mobilization Committee to End the War in Vietnam. The focus of the weekend's events was to demand that President Nixon work quickly to remove troops from Vietnam. At 6:00 p.m. on November 13, 1969, more than forty thousand demonstrators began marching in a single-file line that stretched for miles. A rectangular card around each protester's neck displayed the name of an American soldier killed in Vietnam or the name of a Vietnamese village destroyed or bombed. The marchers started from Arlington National Cemetery in Virginia and crossed over the Memorial Bridge, headed for President Nixon. When each person reached the sidewalk outside the White House, they paused and through a loudspeaker called out the name on their sign, intent on reaching the president's ears in the Oval Office. Less than twenty-four hours later, hundreds of buses would line the sidewalk, separating the president from a disgruntled public.

Still, for almost forty hours, "March against Death" protesters called out the names of people and places senselessly lost before dropping their name card into one of eleven wooden coffins. The last name was placed inside at 7:30 a.m. on November 15, but a few hours later, throngs of demonstrators arrived at the Capitol for the start of a larger anti-war march and rally. Hundreds of thousands of people wanted Nixon to understand they opposed war. Led by three drummers and marching in rows of seventeen that were followed by the eleven coffins, which they intended to deliver to the White House, protesters screamed, "Peace now, peace now!"

Though many pro-war critics waited for violence to erupt as it had at other anti-war demonstrations, the crowds largely practiced the peace they were seeking, supporting the cause with their voices and their feet, not their fists.

Although the war continued for six more years, it was the dedication and resilience of protesters like these that gave Nixon no choice but to ultimately bring the war to a close. It is a reminder that the road to peace is often a long one, but peace is always worth marching for!

EARTH DAY MARCH

Albuquerque, New Mexico, and Nationwide
April 22, 1970

We are going to make people understand that the kind of thing that comes from air pollution and water pollution are the same kinds of things that cause racism, that cause poverty, that cause hunger in this country.

—Arturo Sandoval, Earth Day national committee member, march organizer

Each year, new species of animals are added to the endangered species list. Man in his arrogance appears to think that he can escape that list.

—Senator Gaylord Nelson

TOGETHER WE MARCH TO SAVE OUR ONLY HOME

During the 1960s, groups rallied around a variety of issues, but in April 1970 one in ten Americans came out in support of the same cause—protecting the environment. For many years, the environment had fallen low on most lists of concerns. There were no laws banning toxic waste disposal in rivers and streams, there were few protections for forests and wildlife, and cars and factories were free to pollute the air. Across the country, various groups who did focus on the environment channeled their energies into very specific issues and, unfortunately as a result, only reached small clusters of concerned citizens.

Then in January 1969, when three million gallons of oil flooded into the ocean near Santa Barbara, California, in the most disastrous oil spill in history at the time, thousands of birds and marine life died. Soon after, in June of that same year, the Cuyahoga River in Cleveland, Ohio, caught fire because of toxic waste coating the surface of the water. It was not the first time the river had caught fire, and it would not be the last if the government did not step in to stop factories from using the river as a free and legal dumping ground for their waste. The country started taking notice.

Although a number of Americans were troubled by these well-publicized events, many were still largely unaware of the devastating effect humans themselves played in the problems facing the environment and so weren't moved to action. But Senator Gaylord Nelson of Wisconsin was. He proposed a nationwide teach-in on the environment. Teach-ins, which were started during the anti-war movement to educate students and the public about the war in Vietnam, took their lead from civil rights sit-ins of the 1950s and '60s. Senator Nelson believed teach-ins over the course

APRIL 22
EARTH DAY

of one day in communities across America would be an excellent way to educate the general public on the importance of conservation and taking an active role in caring for the planet.

Americans agreed. The first Earth Day was set for April 22, 1970. Senator Nelson wanted the main energy of the day to come from communities, highlighting the specific issues concerning their areas. That was exactly what university student Arturo Sandoval, one of the main committee members overseeing Earth Day, had in mind too. He wanted the public and politicians to understand that environmental awareness had many layers. It was not just about picking up litter and conserving water, but about understanding *why* these issues persisted.

While other communities planned rallies and cleanups or planted trees, Arturo organized a march through his Barelas neighborhood of Albuquerque, New Mexico. News crews followed behind him and three hundred other Mexican Americans as they traveled down dirt roads and by adobe houses through one of the poorest areas of Albuquerque, where a sewage plant polluted the air and water. Arturo and the other marchers wanted people to be aware that families in lower income communities are more likely to be exposed to harmful pollutants in and around their neighborhoods. They hoped awareness might begin to bring about change. The march wasn't the largest that day, but it was a crucial reminder of the interconnectedness of human issues and those of the natural world, highlighting how our actions and the suffering of others eventually affects each of us.

In addition to Arturo's march, through events organized by one thousand communities, ten thousand schools, and two thousand colleges, an estimated twenty million Americans let politicians know they supported the protection of the environment. In large part due to the energy of these average Americans on the first Earth Day, over the next few years the US government put in place some of the strongest protections for the environment yet, including the Endangered Species Act, the Safe Drinking Water Act, and the formation of the Environmental Protection Agency (EPA), which protects human health and promotes healthy environments.

Although many strides were made in the 1970s, we are still grappling with a multitude of environmental issues—plastic, air and water pollution, waste management, and global climate change. But Earth Day continues each year, reminding us that we can make strides to save the planet, just as they did.

CHRISTOPHER STREET LIBERATION DAY MARCH

New York, New York
June 28, 1970

Now we've walked in the open and know how pleasant it is to have self-respect and to be treated as citizens and human beings. . . . We want to stay in the sunlight from now on.

—Dick Leitsch, LGBT rights activist

TOGETHER WE MARCH TO LOVE WHOM WE WANT

The year 1969 wasn't the first time police had raided the Stonewall Inn in New York City's Greenwich Village, and it wouldn't be the last. But it was one of the first times patrons fought back.

Like many other marginalized communities in the United States and abroad during that period, the LGBTQ community experienced discrimination and hatred in public spaces. Gay people were not always free to be themselves socially, and they often faced economic discrimination. Almost every state had laws against same-sex relationships, people of the same sex dancing together, or wearing articles of clothing meant for the opposite sex. But unlike at some establishments, there were never signs outside the Stonewall that read, "If you are gay, please stay away." Stonewall Inn was a haven for the gay community, but it also accepted patrons often shunned by that community—homeless teens who'd run away or been kicked out by parents for being gay, transgender people, and gay people of color. Especially for them, the Stonewall was home.

So, on June 28, 1969, when the police raided the bar for the second time in a matter of days, patrons had had enough. Many felt their place of refuge was being targeted not simply because it served alcohol illegally after having been denied a liquor license because it was a gay bar, but simply because of who its patrons were. Instead

SAY IT CLEAR
SAY IT LOUD
GAY IS GOOD AND
GAY IS PROUD!

of running for cover as they often did, patrons decided to speak up and defend the bar that welcomed them in.

Soon police found themselves overwhelmed outside the bar by angered Stonewall regulars and their supporters in the community. It took hundreds of police several hours to clear the crowds, but for six days the LGBTQ community came back to protest by holding hands, dancing together, and kissing in public—something most had never dared do in the open. For many, it was a turning point for the LGBTQ rights movement.

Stonewall spurred a group of committed gay activists, already fighting for equal rights, to become even more vocal and forceful in their demands for change. A year later, they got together to plan a memorial parade in New York City. It was a day for remembrance and for demanding fundamental human rights and protection against police harassment and employment discrimination. But it was also a day of liberation, about finally being seen rather than hiding.

When the march began, a few hundred people started off from Christopher Street, holding a Christopher Street Gay Liberation Day banner. Even though many gathered on the sidewalks to gawk or show support, initially the street itself was not filled with marchers. However, as they progressed up Sixth Avenue toward Central Park chanting, "Say it loud, we're gay and proud," people started to shed their fears and apprehensions and join the movement. By the time the procession reached Central Park, it stretched fifteen city blocks. People held hands, waved, laughed, and chanted. Police turned their backs on the marchers to show their disregard, but the LGBTQ community and their supporters were determined to keep going in order to help cause social change for them. Never before had so many gay and lesbian people gathered together in public for a common cause.

Within the first few years after the uprising and parade, hundreds of gay and lesbian organizations formed around the country to further build the movement, increasing the visibility necessary for change. A decade later, large corporations finally created policies against employment discrimination based on sexual orientation, and in 2015, the US Supreme Court made same-sex marriage legal nationwide. Although much was accomplished, there is still work to be done in support of LGBTQ rights, and this one-time event to encourage gay pride has become a yearly month-long celebration held all around the world to continue this work. The Christopher Street Liberation Day parade, now known as the NYC Pride March, attracts millions of people worldwide each year. In the US, June is now LGBTQ Pride Month. What started as a small rebellion in one New York bar helped spark a globally visible movement in large part because people stepped out of the shadows together.

Christopher St

THE LONGEST WALK

San Francisco, California, to Washington, DC
February 11–July 15, 1978

On this walk I learned that people with a belief in something can overcome mountains.

—Lehman Brightman, American Indian Movement,
one of the organizers of the Longest Walk

TOGETHER WE MARCH TO PRESERVE OUR CULTURE AND OUR LANDS

In the 1970s, while the LGBTQ community marched for their future, Native Americans fought to have treaty agreements and other legal promises of the past protected. Since Christopher Columbus and other colonizers first stepped on the shores of what is now called the Americas, First Peoples, who have always inhabited these lands, have been in an ongoing struggle to preserve their rights to it.

When European settlers first arrived, Indigenous communities allowed them entry, and taught them how to farm and survive. But colonists kept coming. They illegally claimed more and more land that already belonged to millions of original peoples, citizens with their own independent governments. By the early 1800s, Indigenous peoples, lumped together, were further brutalized by the federal Indian Removal Act and ordered to sign away their rightful territories and relocate to areas far from their beloved homelands, where they could be corralled and controlled. Indigenous peoples resisted and were forcibly removed from their homes, farms, and communities. They were marched at gunpoint by the US military across mountains and rivers on "long walks." There was little food, clothing, and shelter; thousands died in the harsh winters. White settlers moved into their homes and took over their thriving farms and businesses.

The lands that Indigenous people were forced onto began to be called reservations; more treaties were signed. Some treaties in the late 1800s acknowledged that these lands were indeed sovereign nations and were to be governed by Indigenous peoples. However, the US government never honored any of the five hundred treaties, although Indigenous peoples upheld their end of the bargain. Over the next two centuries, Indigenous lands were decreased more and more.

In 1978, when eleven bills were brought before Congress that threatened Indigenous peoples' sovereign rights once more, many Native Americans refused to let it happen again. If these bills passed, they would limit Indigenous peoples' water, fishing, and hunting rights, as well as the First Peoples' ability to self-govern. First Nations activists knew the media would not bring attention to these bills without impetus, and they needed to act. Organizers recalled the cruel and forced "long walks" of their ancestors and felt another "long walk" would be just the venue needed to educate the world about the injustices.

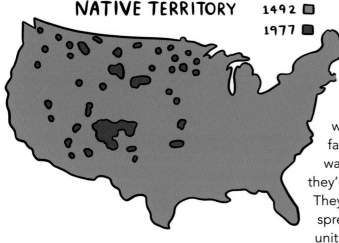

NATIVE TERRITORY   1492 ■
                    1977 ■

Supported by more than one hundred tribal nations and encouraged by the Black Power movement and similar protests of the period, the American Indian Movement (AIM) organized a three-thousand-mile spiritual walk from the West Coast to Washington, DC, to raise public awareness of these bills, to get a meeting with President Carter, and to connect with who they were spiritually and as a cultural people. Similar to the farm workers of Delano, they wanted to educate people along the way about the conditions indigenous people faced, the "long walks" they'd been forced to take, and the strength of their cultural heritage. They also hoped the walk would bring the various tribes, which were spread across different reservations and urban areas, closer together, uniting the voice behind their demands.

They started with two dozen marchers, but thousands of supporters joined them along the way, some walking across only one state, others keeping stride with the dedicated group for days. They braved blizzards and tornadoes as well as blisters and sore muscles. A caravan of pickup trucks and station wagons drove the elderly and the very young, while also providing shelter and relief for others who needed it during the journey. They held informational rallies and slept in tents, school buildings, gyms, churches, or fairgrounds. They carried no posters, only banners, flags, staffs with eagle feathers, and a sacred pipe as they crossed some of the original Indigenous routes through Utah, Kansas, Illinois, West Virginia, and Maryland. And people from many different backgrounds marched in support with their First Nations brothers and sisters, like the Japanese Buddhist monks who made the trek, adding their drums and prayers to those of the Indigenous marchers.

After five months of braving the elements, lack of food, and aggressive shouts from opposition, the marchers arrived in DC to cheers, whoops, and honking horns. The two dozen original walkers had blossomed to more than two thousand participants. Even though they did not get to meet with President Carter, they deemed the walk a success. Almost two dozen dedicated marchers completed the entire journey, which had increased their Indigenous pride and energized their movement, and the eleven bills did not pass in Congress. Many marchers believe the walk led to the passage of the American Indian Religious Freedom Act in August 1978, which preserved their cultural rights and protected their religious traditions. Indigenous Americans are still fighting to preserve their lands and improve their communities and have held the Longest Walk several times since 1978. It is a shining example that marches don't end after the last step, and we must continue to stand together to protect vulnerable communities.

CAPE TOWN PEACE MARCH

Cape Town, South Africa
September 13, 1989

**Nothing, nothing can overwhelm the spirit of a people that yearn
to be free. They are unstoppable.**

—Archbishop Desmond Tutu

TOGETHER WE MARCH TO END RACIAL SEPARATENESS AND A DIVIDED NATION

Just as Native Americans were forced from their ancestral lands in America, in 1913 many Blacks in South Africa were forcibly stripped of most of their land and their ability to make a livelihood, despite being the majority in the population. In most areas they were also not afforded the right to vote to change the laws and rulers who oppressed them.

After World War II, things worsened. The all-white National Party, made up of Afrikaners, an ethnic group descended from Western Europeans, came into power and established even more racial segregation through an "apartness" that became known as "apartheid." By 1950, Black Africans, mixed race (called "Coloured" at that time), Indian, and Asian peoples all stood separate from whites under the law. Much like segregation in the American South, soon signs labeled WHITE ONLY appeared in all public areas.

Since they did not have a true voice in government, Black South Africans had formed their own organizations to combat injustice, including the African National Congress (ANC); as apartheid was established, the ANC was at the forefront of the resistance. Threatened by the strength of this resistance and the unrest, the Afrikaner government banned the ANC and similar organizations, and arrested leading activists including Nelson Mandela.

ARCHBISHOP DESMOND TUTU

By 1989, with pressure building from the outside world and within the country, the National Party began to fracture, but anti-apartheid groups became stronger, joining together to form the United Democratic Front (UDF). For more than three years, the country had been in a state of emergency, banning political protests in an attempt to tamp down the voices calling for equality. But the people protested anyway. All over the nation, groups from different backgrounds boarded buses and had picnics on the beach together, while Blacks also went to white-only hospitals to be treated. They all defied apartheid laws in a civil and organized defiance campaign. In response, a peaceful march was broken up by police using a water cannon, and just days later more than twenty people were killed when police broke up an election-day demonstration. But Archbishop Desmond Tutu, the 1984 Nobel Peace laureate, was

not deterred, saying, "We are going to defy until freedom comes." When he called for another march, people across the country were willing, despite the ongoing violence.

On September 13, 1989, more than 20,000 people of all ethnic groups showed up to march in Cape Town, defying the ban and apartheid. They were ready to march without permission, but after increasing threats of global isolation, financial losses because of international sanctions, and the unyielding fight of the people, acting President de Klerk relented and allowed the protest.

At that time, the march may not have seemed historic in certain parts of the world, but in South Africa it was the first anti-apartheid march to be given permission by the government in three years and the first near Parliament in over twenty years. Religious, civic, and community leaders led by Archbishop Tutu organized the event, while people of all backgrounds, including hundreds of white people, were on hand to show they did not want to be separated. Leaders representing different organizations locked arms, leading the way from St. George's Cathedral to City Hall. The march was a call for peace and equality, an inclusive governing body, the release of imprisoned activist leaders, and a lift on the bans against anti-apartheid organizations meeting. The people wanted a new, nonsegregated, and just South Africa. This time there were no growling dogs or police in riot gear with tear gas. The government did not want a show of violence while the world watched again. Instead the flag of the outlawed African National Congress (ANC) waved overhead as the crowd chanted for new leadership along the mile-long route.

NELSON MANDELA

Through marching together, a multitude of South Africans showed their collective power, and the acting president vowed at last to come to the table with all involved. It was one of the largest permitted marches in South African history. With continued pressure, five months later, Nelson Mandela was released from prison after twenty-seven years, and finally, five years later in 1994, apartheid was officially outlawed. Nelson Mandela became the first president elected in an open and democratic election by the people of South Africa, all because individuals came together to march against being kept apart.

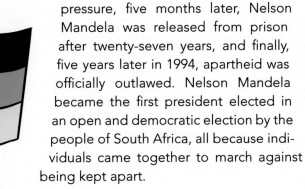

CAPITOL CRAWL

The greatest lesson of the civil rights movement is that the moment you let others speak for you, you lose.

—Ed Roberts, first student who used a wheelchair
at University of California, Berkeley

TOGETHER WE MARCH TO ELIMINATE BARRIERS BOTH MENTAL AND PHYSICAL

Many people do not think twice about climbing a step or answering a telephone. For centuries though, disabled Americans have experienced countless daily barriers that limit their independence in small tasks such as these and place legal restrictions upon their freedoms and their ability to act independently.

Like other marginalized groups, people with physical and mental disabilities wanted fair and equal access to society, including an end to discrimination in education, employment, and government services, and accommodated access to buses, trains, and planes. They did not want to have everything in their lives decided for them. They knew that their disabilities did not mean they were incapable of being an active part of the conversations concerning their own lives.

While the disability rights movement that formed in the 1960s made significant strides at the federal level by the 1970s, the laws did nothing to improve access to privately owned restaurants, stores, telephone and television services, offices, movie theaters, and more. So disabled citizens made their presence—and the disadvantages they faced daily—known to the public through civil disobedience. They blocked inaccessible buses and buildings with their wheelchairs and bodies, they had wheel-ins and sit-ins, they held public hearings, and they sent letters to congressmen. Leaders pressed for more unity, and people with differing disabilities committed to fighting for one another until laws would be passed to protect them all from discrimination.

This call for unity led to the proposal of the Americans with Disabilities Act (ADA), which would give all disabled people the same civil rights and access afforded to other minority groups.

By March 1990, though, the passage of the ADA was stalled in the House of Representatives as public transit companies lobbied against the expensive renovations the accessibility requirements dictated. But disability activists were determined not to let the

bill be weakened. They knew they needed to go to Washington, DC, to fight. Yet, for many, traveling wasn't a possibility due to these accessibility limitations. While those who could not attend sent their support through letters and telegrams to Congress, American Disabled for Attendant Programs Today (ADAPT), a disability rights group, organized events for protesters who could.

On March 12, 1990, about one thousand disabled people and their families headed to Washington, DC. They marched and rolled down Pennsylvania Avenue to the steps of the US Capitol, waving signs demanding, ACCESS! They rallied at the foot of the Capitol, and then together sixty protesters dropped their crutches, walkers, and canes or left their wheelchairs behind to crawl, roll, or pull themselves up the more than seventy-five steps to the building, in the district's first crawl-in. They knew other Americans needed to witness the barriers they faced each day. The activists did not want sympathy; they crawled for fairness and action. The youngest crawler, eight-year-old Jennifer Keelan, who has cerebral palsy, refused to stop, declaring "I'll take all night if I have to!"

The American public and politicians watched, moved by her efforts and those of the other demonstrators. Their willingness to act helped shift what was once accepted. Combined with similar efforts across the country, this event helped ensure that the ADA passed in the House without becoming weakened. Among other things, the law requires flat or ramped entrances to buildings, accessible parking spaces, and telephone services for the hearing and speech impaired. It also protects disabled people from job discrimination. Although some disagreed with the protesters' tactics during the crawl-in, no one could disagree that they were noticed and heard. Four months later, when President George H. W. Bush signed the ADA into law, he said, "Let the shameful wall of exclusion finally come tumbling down."

Even though many strides have been made since the passage of the ADA, like other fights for civil rights, all is still not equal. People with disabilities still experience discrimination and strive to be hired as capable workers deserving of equal pay and positions, and there are still companies and services unwilling to make changes to ensure equal access for every American. So people with disabilities and their allies will continue to come together to march, roll, crawl, and demand until full access to society for everyone is a reality.

GLOBAL MARCH AGAINST CHILD LABOUR

Manila, Philippines; Geneva, Switzerland; and Worldwide
January 17–June 1, 1998

My whole life has just one single aim, that is to restore childhood. That is to restore freedom.

—Kailash Satyarthi

TOGETHER WE MARCH TO END CHILD EXPLOITATION

We think of child labor as a thing of the past, from the time of the mill children of Pennsylvania. Despite the attention that protest garnered, to this day, all over the world, some children are still forced to work in unsafe conditions when they are very young, resulting in numerous health issues, injuries, stunted physical or mental development, and even death.

A number of these children have never had the opportunity to get an education, and for many of them, there are no other options. Much like Mother Jones, there are people and organizations still trying to help give them a future. In the early 1990s, after a successful five-month child labor protest march across India, longtime child labor activist and 2014 Nobel Laureate Kailash Satyarthi asked a group of young Indian labor marchers what they wanted to do next. Their response was simple and immediate—children are not only exploited in India, they said, they face exploitation in every corner of the world. The children wanted a global march.

Only a few years later, with the help of one thousand organizations—including some led by teachers—from more than one hundred countries, they created the Global March against Child Labour. The march would take place over many months and be led by young laborers around the world demanding, "No more tools in tiny hands. We want books. We want toys!"

KAILASH SATYARTHI

On January 17, 1998, hundreds of demonstrators set out from Manila in the Philippines, walking miles for an end to child labor. Then a core group flew to Thailand to continue the fight, marching with locals across Asia. Car caravans and planes bridged the gap between countries for some involved, transporting them between marches so they could keep the message alive across the globe. Along the way, former child laborers and activists held teach-ins, like the ones used on Earth Day, to educate the public about the atrocities of child labor and to explain why it was important for people to care and act. They hoped to bring worldwide awareness to the fact that child labor was happening now, not just in the past, and to emphasize specific problems facing children in different countries.

In February, another committed group started in Brazil on a route across the Americas that would take them through Mexico City, Los Angeles, and Washington, DC. In March and April other groups marched through countries in Africa including South Africa, Kenya, and Nigeria. Seventy-one heads of state and dignitaries across the globe joined portions of the march, including kings, queens, presidents, and prime ministers. And finally, in late May, select groups from across the globe flew to Europe for the remaining leg of the march. Coming together, they raised their fists, banners, flags, and voices as they marched to Geneva, Switzerland, and the International Labour Organization (ILO) conference, where a new global pact against child labor was being considered.

Marchers wanted governments of the world to establish and enforce laws that would protect vulnerable children and their right to an education everywhere. They especially wanted to put an end to the worst, most harmful, and hidden types of child labor—including prostitution, child soldiers, slavery, and other hazardous work. Marchers collectively trekked almost 50,000 miles, braving the elements and rough areas in 103 countries, aiming for the Geneva committee to see them and draft an international law to protect their childhood. By uniting, these young people began to understand that their numbers would force people to listen to them.

CHILDREN TO SCHOOL ADULTS TO WORK EXPLOITERS TO JAIL

And they did! At the ILO conference, the organization drafted Convention No. 182, which states that a country is committed to protecting children under eighteen and must immediately end the "worst forms of child labor." The following year it was unanimously adopted by members of the ILO, and the overall number of child laborers has decreased ever since. The Global March was one of the largest and most successful efforts in history for children's rights, but until every child has the freedom to play and to go to school, the fight is far from over.

MILLION PUPPET MARCH

Washington, DC
November 3, 2012

This is all about really deciding who and what we are as a country. If we make a statement that the arts, public television, and public radio are important to us, that says something about us, and if we say that they should be forfeited, that says something about us.

—Million Puppet Marcher from "Million Puppet March Documentary—2012"

TOGETHER WE MARCH FOR OUR EDUCATION

Did Big Bird teach you letters? Or did the Count make numbers fun? Do you know more about your neighborhood because of the neighbors you met on *Sesame Street*? For more than six million viewers each week, *Sesame Street* is where kids can learn about our world from trusted characters who feel like friends.

But not everyone values these lessons. When 2012 presidential candidate Mitt Romney said that he liked PBS and loved Big Bird, but that he wasn't going to keep spending money on them, he assumed federally funding the Public Broadcasting Service (PBS) that brings us beloved characters like Big Bird was an unnecessary expense for American taxpayers.

Hundreds of Americans instantly disagreed. In 2012, public broadcasting was part of the lives of 170 million Americans, and PBS was rated the Most Trusted Institution in the United States. In his comments, Romney had also crucially overlooked public broadcasting's power as "America's largest classroom." Shows like *Sesame Street* were created not only to show the very young an inclusive world where everyone is valued, but to even the playing field for almost half of the nation's three- to four-year-olds who do not attend preschool or Head Start programs. The money to support public broadcasting basically costs each taxpayer $1.35 per year, less than a cup of coffee, but if this funding was lost, many of the local TV and radio stations that carried this con-

tent would be lost too. As a result, many understood Romney's proposed cut would affect more than just Big Bird. It would directly impact rural areas, the very young, low-income families, the elderly, minority groups, and teachers.

Within seconds, people across the country expressed their desire to #SaveBigBird on social media. Seventeen thousand tweets per minute referenced Big Bird, ten thousand mentioned PBS, and on Google "Big Bird" was the "fourth-highest-rising" search among users. Mitt Romney had ruffled feathers! For college student Chris Mecham and animation executive Michael Bellavia, this was about more than a hashtag and a bottom line. The two men did not know each other, but they shared a similar goal—to protect Big Bird and public broadcasting. Bellavia quickly bought MillionMuppetMarch.com, only to find someone miles away who'd had a similar idea. A Facebook page Mecham created moments after Romney's comments quickly gained hundreds of likes, and two concerned citizens suddenly became novice organizers.

Unlike the way the Women Strike for Peace had to use Christmas card lists, or how the March on Washington organizers wrote thousands of letters, the internet got the message to the world in lightning speed, and people responded. The Million Puppet March organizers encouraged everyone to show up in Washington, DC, three days before the presidential election with their "best fuzzy, feathered, felted friends" to show "support for Big Bird, puppets, PBS and all that is good." For over forty years, public broadcasting had served the public, now the public was ready to serve it!

It was time to march. On November 3, starting from Lincoln Park, almost one thousand people, puppets, and Muppets from across America joined together to head for the Capitol reflecting pool, chanting "Know Puppets, Know Peace!" They also sang a classic line from the *Mister Rogers' Neighborhood* show, "Won't you be my neighbor?" Those who couldn't reach DC participated online as part of the Virtual Million Puppet March. They uploaded videos on a Million Puppets YouTube channel to lend their support to the in-person marchers. After the march, there was a festive atmosphere filled with skits, puppet shows, and music where people celebrated what they had learned from public broadcasting.

Like many of the marches before it, a group of concerned citizens took the steps to help stop an injustice from happening. Although *Sesame Street* became part of HBO's subscription service in 2015, where paying subscribers have a nine-month head start on new episodes, federal funds were not withdrawn from public broadcasting, and there is still much educational programming produced there for children and teachers to enjoy. Because of these marchers, Americans and government leaders were reminded that public broadcasting isn't a wasted luxury, but is essential at all levels of society as it gives us a well-rounded glimpse into the multitude of American experiences. That day hundreds remembered through marching what being a good neighbor was all about.

WANYAMA URITHI WETU WALK
("WILDLIFE IS OUR HERITAGE" WALK)

Nairobi, Kenya
January 22, 2013

We don't want to wait till the day that there is one elephant standing in Kenya. We want to take action now.

—Nyokabi Gethaiga, founder of the Let Live movement

TOGETHER WE MARCH TO SAVE OUR ANIMAL FRIENDS

For millions of years, elephants have roamed the earth, journeying within the forests and savannas of Africa and Asia. They are a majestic species that value friendship and familial bonds. The matriarchs teach the young how to survive, navigate rough terrain, confront danger as a defense, and use their impressive memories to lead the way to the best watering holes. However, they have little chance of defending themselves against certain enemies, including humans.

In the 1800s, western traders valued elephants' gleaming tusks of ivory, calling it "white gold." Soon there was a demand, and people from across the globe came to Africa, because unlike Asian elephants, both male and female African elephants have tusks. Some people came not only to admire the great animals in their natural habitat, but to kill them for these mighty tusks. People wanted ivory for many things, including combs, jewelry, piano keys, and pool balls, but there was little concern for the gentle giants they killed in order to meet this great demand. In the early 1900s there were more than ten million African elephants, but by 1979 there were little more than a million. Between 1979 and 1989 alone, humans wiped out half of all African elephants and only 600,000 elephants remained. Conservationists and governments worried. Action was needed or the majestic creatures would soon be extinct!

The Convention on International Trade in Endangered Species of Wild Fauna and Flora (CITES) responded by placing African elephants on its most endangered species list in 1976, joining Asian elephants that had been listed since 1975, but they were still hunted. Even with government bans, the penalties and jail times for poaching were far less severe than those for drugs, guns, or human trafficking, so poachers were not deterred by the risks of breaking the law. The ivory trade continued to boom, and elephants continued to suffer.

This escalated until January 2013, when a family of eleven elephants were gunned down for their tusks. It was the single largest killing of elephants ever to occur in Kenya, and Kenyans were outraged. Wildlife activists demanded urgent action. Kenyan citizens, human rights advocates, celebrities, artists, media personalities, and conservationists joined forces to create Kenyans United Against Poaching (KUAPO). They were ready to march for the elephants and demand that poaching be considered a national disaster. They wanted harsher punishments for poachers, stronger legislation, global awareness, and support.

On January 13, they marched through the streets of Nairobi, weaving in and out of traffic, with slogans painted on their arms and faces, declaring "Blood Ivory" and "Save the elephants!" It wasn't simply an animal rights issue anymore, it was an environmental issue and human rights issue as well. Poaching harmed animals, which affected ecosystems, altering daily life and tourism. It affected the world! Protesters' roughly four-mile walk may have started on the streets of Kenya, but through digital outreach, local action, and a collaborative effort between KUAPO, the Sheldrick Wildlife Trust, and others, that one march grew a year later into the Global March for Elephants and Rhinos. It took place on World Animal Day in October 2014 on six continents, in 136 cities, including Nairobi, New York, Soweto, Paris, Vancouver, Tokyo, Amsterdam, and Washington, DC. With signs declaring, EXTINCTION IS FOREVER! and hands marked with the words LET LIVE, people came together and marched in even greater numbers.

While they raised much global awareness, the work is far from over. Poaching has decreased in some countries, but remains a threat in others. To protect these animals from possible extinction in our generation, the Global March for Elephants and Rhinos continues around the world today. When asked what needed to be done internationally, President Ali Bongo Ondimba of Gabon said it best: "Let's kill the [ivory] market, and we'll save the animals. We'll save also human beings." Only then will the animals we share this earth with be truly safe. Until then, we must continue to march for them and us.

SECOND YEAR OF MARCH

NAACP YOUTH MARCH

Ferguson, Missouri
August 23, 2014

It means a lot to me personally that we break this cycle of violence, defuse tension, and build trust.

—Capt. Ronald Johnson of Missouri Highway Patrol

TOGETHER WE MARCH FOR BLACK LIVES TO MATTER

In 1965, when Jimmie Lee Jackson was shot by a police officer during a peaceful march in Marion, Alabama, Black citizens united to march from Selma to Montgomery. The six hundred marchers, who had broken no laws, were soon met by state troopers wielding nightsticks and tear gas. Marchers only wanted protection under the law for all people, but realized they were not even afforded protection in the streets by their own community police force.

It was not the first time some police officers stood in the way of peaceful marches for progress and free speech, and, unfortunately, it would not be the last. While police officers work hard to keep us safe and maintain order, sometimes this protection is not equal and can even be used to falsely justify brutality and intimidation against others. No group has experienced this more than the Black community. The tense relationship between law enforcement and the Black community began during slavery and the Jim Crow era, but did not exist only in the South nor end with civil rights.

So, on August 9, 2014, when eighteen-year-old Michael Brown was fatally shot by a police officer in Ferguson, Missouri, the Black community was frustrated, angered, and saddened, but not surprised. Darren Wilson, a white officer, claimed Brown reached into his police car, so he shot him in self-defense. But witnesses told varying stories. Either way, Brown was an unarmed teen, and for people in Ferguson and the Black community at large, they saw yet another unarmed Black person killed needlessly.

The Ferguson community erupted. Some looted, but most marched, shouted, and cried, joining others in the streets, night after night in protest. They refused to let this tragedy go ignored. But even those protesting peacefully found themselves confronted by militarized police with tear gas, flash grenades, and rubber bullets.

Back in 2013—a year after another unarmed Black teen, Trayvon Martin, had been fatally shot and his killer was acquitted—Alicia Garza,

BLACK LIVES MATTER

Hands UP DON'T SHOOT

one of the co-founders of the Black Lives Matter movement, a group that speaks out about violence against Black people, wrote on Facebook, "I continue to be surprised at how little Black lives matter." This sparked a tweet from Los Angeles based community organizer Patrisse Khan-Cullors: #BlackLivesMatter, which garnered a tremendous response. Weeks after the Michael Brown killing, people in Ferguson agreed. They were ready to show just how much Black life *did* matter to them. Many understood fatal killings like this were happening all across America, and they couldn't be silent anymore, even with the heavy police presence. Soon the eyes of the country were on Ferguson, and the epidemic of police shootings of unarmed Black people was in the forefront of the nation's mind.

Finally, on August 23, after weeks of unrest, the St. Louis County chapter of the NAACP organized an official youth march through Ferguson to help young people turn some of their frustrations into action. Leaders knew it was vital for everyone to refocus their anger. Activism was what was needed instead. So, after most of the news media had gone, hundreds of young people came to Ferguson to march. Many wore bright T-shirts with a quote from Roslyn M. Brock, NAACP Board of Directors Chairman Emeritus, that read COURAGE WILL NOT SKIP THIS GENERATION. And with every step they took together, their courage got stronger. At first, they walked in silence in remembrance and as a call for peace; then, borrowing the beat from a 1990s rap song, they chanted, "Ain't no power like the people's power. Because the people's power will vote!" Although the march was for the young, older marchers both white and Black joined the procession up and down a half-mile stretch in Ferguson.

This time the response by police was much different. They helped lead the way in regular uniforms not riot gear, whether holding up an NAACP banner out in front or marching hand in hand with the young. In order to move forward and correct the wrongs of the past, they understood everyone needed to come together, march together, and demand justice for all together.

Since the Ferguson shooting, the killing of Black people by police has not ceased. But in response, communities across the country are following in Ferguson's footsteps with demonstrations, rallies, and marches. People refuse to stay silent. The Black Lives Matter movement now has forty member-led chapters worldwide, and it continues to grow, ignited by small marches and a drive to seek an end to racial violence.

WOMEN'S MARCH

Washington, DC, and Worldwide
January 21, 2017

We join in diversity to show our presence in numbers too great to ignore . . . women's rights are human rights. We stand together, recognizing that defending the most marginalized among us is defending all of us.

—Women's March 2017 "Mission & Vision"

TOGETHER WE MARCH IN UNITY FOR ALL WOMEN'S RIGHTS

Long before suffragists in England trudged through mud in 1907 demanding the vote, or women in America fought for liberation beginning in the 1960s, Abigail Adams, wife and personal advisor to John Adams, one of America's Founding Fathers, implored her husband to "remember the ladies." She understood how vital it was for women to have protections under the law, and she warned, "If particular care and attention is not paid to the ladies, we are determined to foment a rebellion, and will not hold ourselves bound by any laws in which we have no voice, or representation."

More than two hundred years later, her words continue to ring true. In almost every aspect of life, women still fight for equality, and the right to make choices for themselves. They are confronted with barriers and metaphorical glass ceilings, leaving them stalled and underrepresented in the upper ranks of academia, corporate America, the tech world, and in political life. Sexual and domestic violence are still real everyday fears for many women, and women are also engaged in a constant fight for adequate health care, birth control, childcare, and family-leave benefits. Women of color and poor, transgender, bisexual, queer, disabled, immigrant, and indigenous women fare even worse in these areas.

While earlier women's movements had made strides, at the end of 2016, many women felt the gains they had made in this struggle were in danger of being yanked away by policies threatened by the incoming administration. In online chat groups, women expressed their shock, frustration, and anger about where they believed their rights and the country would soon be headed under the incoming administration. Beginning as a single Facebook post, "I think we should march!" turned into a rallying cry overnight, endorsed online by more than 300,000 women and their supporters, who were eager to join a collective movement. Women were ready to march to let political leaders and the world know that equal pay, freedom from violence, the ability to govern their own bodies, and other women's rights were issues that mattered to them.

MAKE AMERICA THINK AGAIN

fight like a girl

SILENCE WILL NOT PROTECT YOU

MY BODY MY CHOICE

too many issues for one sign

women's rights are HUMAN RIGHTS

"We may not have chosen the time, but the time has chosen us." —John Lewis

girls just wanna have FUNdamental rights

The aim of the Women's March organizers was to be inclusive, calling on women from all backgrounds, religious affiliations, economic classes, and geographic locations to march together. The march would fight for a woman's right to education, property, work, and equal rights in family law, but organizers also understood these rights intersected fundamentally with a number of other causes they cared about, such as racial injustice, disability rights, immigration rights, and LGBTQIA+ rights. They were ready to speak for them all.

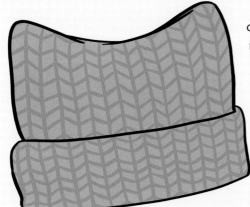

The date was set for one day after the inauguration of America's forty-fifth president. The morning of January 21, 2017, organizers expected a crowd of 200,000, but nearly half a million people showed up! People from all over the country journeyed to Washington, DC, many donning pink clothing and pink hats, making a powerful visual statement. Celebrities and politicians joined the voices of thousands as they marched along the National Mall, headed for the Washington Monument, with thousands of signs displaying their frustrations to the world. Protesters hoped to trigger a resistance movement against messages of hate. Their message was carried all over as 673 sister marches took place across the country and 261 marches were held internationally. Worldwide, more than five million people got involved.

As with so many marches before, participants learned that everyone has the power and ability to resist in their own communities, not just at big events, but also by voting. The call for voter turnout was answered, and the 2018 midterm elections led to many historic wins by female candidates.

However, other politicians continue to threaten the rights of women, so the fight is not over. Women's marches occur each year, bringing women together to protect their rights and those of other vulnerable groups in their own families and communities. Women and their allies will continue to march together to remind those in power and the whole world to "remember the ladies."

THE WALK TO STAY HOME:
A JOURNEY OF HOPE

New York, New York, to Washington, DC
February 15–March 1, 2018

We walk in community for our community.

—Hector Jairo Martinez, The Walk to Stay Home marcher

TOGETHER WE MARCH TO DECLARE OUR HOME

"I went down to the capital and I / took back what they stole from me and I / took back my dignity and I / took back my humanity . . ."

Throughout history, these words could have been spoken by so many who marched, sacrificed, and struggled for freedom and inclusion. But in 2018, they were uttered from the hearts of a group of young people, known as DREAMers, committed to coming out of the shadows to speak for themselves and the over eleven million undocumented immigrants living on the margins of America, trying to make a better life for themselves and their families.

Back in 2001, lawmakers introduced a bill in Congress known as the Development, Relief and Education for Alien Minors Act (DREAM). It would afford some undocumented minors brought to the US illegally when they were young, through no fault of their own, the ability to seek higher education, obtain a driver's license, and get a job. But unfortunately, many versions of the bill failed to pass through Congress, leaving these young people living with uncertainty.

It wasn't until 2012, when President Barack Obama issued an executive order, that certain undocumented children were granted protection from possible deportation to countries many of them hardly knew. The Deferred Action for Childhood Arrivals (DACA) was not a perfect or permanent solution, but it was a start, and many of the young people, or DREAMers, it would benefit refused to get discouraged.

Development **R**elief and **E**ducation for **A**lien **M**inors Act

But just five years later, on September 5, 2017, after President Obama left office, the DACA program was ended. No more applications would be taken, and only a small number of DACA recipients could apply for the two-year renewal. This left thousands of young immigrants' futures at risk. Lawmakers were given six months to find a solution, but there was much doubt they would. That is when the Seed Project, a nonviolent organization fighting for permanent protections for undocumented youth, believed it was time to rally together and have a symbolic walk—The Walk to Stay Home: A Journey of Hope. Much like the Longest Walk and other multiday marches, the more ground the undocumented young people and their supporters covered, the more attention they would garner for their fight.

Many of them had always felt like statistics, not people. But now it was time to tell their stories. They needed to show why it was so important to pass a "clean" DREAM Act that gave them the opportunity to become citizens of the country they have always called home, without harming others in immigrant communities in the process. Along the 250-mile walk from New York to Washington, DC, they needed to change the minds of unaccepting people in the community and shift lawmakers into more aggressive action to protect them.

Eleven marchers were chosen to symbolize each of the eleven million undocumented voices that often go unheard, or else are vilified in the news. Most of the marchers were in their twenties, and had come from all over the country to protest for the right to stay. They worked together to make it through, sharing the stories behind their statistics at rallies, and shouting out their future hopes. The march was long and grueling but as one marcher, Hector J. Martinez, said, "We will take a chance, because our community is worth fighting for." They slept in churches and relied on the generosity of strangers along the arduous walk. It took fifteen days, walking an average of eighteen miles a day, on highway shoulders, unpaved paths, and sidewalks, but they made it to Washington—together. Full of uncertainty and hope, they were determined to be seen and heard, even while many lawmakers continued to push their concerns to the side. They had come a long way for their right to stay home.

Though many in the nation heard the stories of these DREAMers, DACA's future is still uncertain. The mission statement of the United States Citizenship and Immigration Services no longer refers to the United States as a "nation of immigrants," and instead of welcoming people, there are movements to detain and ban more and more groups of people who come here seeking refuge and better lives. So the DREAMers and their supporters will continue to fight for everything they marched for until Congress steps in to protect this vulnerable population that contributes so much to America.

BUILD BRIDGES NOT WALLS

MARCH FOR OUR LIVES

Washington, DC, and Worldwide
March 24, 2018

**We are the turn of this century. We are the voice for change.
We are the pieces to fix what America is falling short on.**

—Mya Middleton, March for Our Lives speaker

TOGETHER WE MARCH BECAUSE PEOPLE MATTER MORE THAN GUNS

Across America, students should be thinking about their schoolwork, but instead some have found themselves ducking under desks and running for their lives. In recent history, mass shootings have become a terrifying and frequent reality in America. Columbine High School, Virginia Tech, and Sandy Hook Elementary School are known nationwide, not because they are home to the country's best debate team or football champions, but because some of the most tragic mass shootings in US history took place on their grounds.

After each shooting, the call for gun control got stronger around the country; however, it was not loud enough to compete with the voices defending people's Second Amendment right to possess firearms—gun lobbyists like the National Rifle Association, politicians financially supported by them, and gun owners. Each time people promised never again; each time nothing changed.

But in 2018, survivors of a school shooting at Marjory Stoneman Douglas High School in Parkland, Florida, pushed back their grief and acted. After seventeen of their classmates and school staff members were killed by a nineteen-year-old gunman, the students were angered by how easily he could legally buy an assault rifle and destroy lives. Immediately, they demanded change. They used social media, television, radio and newspaper interviews, and opinion pieces to get their message heard. #NeverAgain, #March4OurLives, and #DouglasStrong became their hashtag rallying cries.

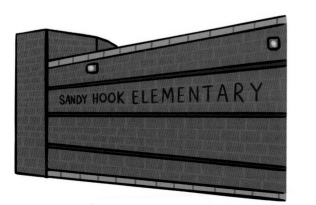

They felt strongly that only state and national gun law reform would prevent this from happening again to another school or group of people. They did not want condolences, apologies, and prayers. They wanted action and they didn't trust their futures to those who hadn't yet done anything to protect them. Within a little over a week, the students themselves met with Florida lawmakers and began to plan their first step—a march.

In one student's living room, the teens organized. Parkland survivors Cameron Kasky, Emma González, David Hogg, Jaclyn Corin, Alex Wind, and Ryan Deitsch took the lead, with the help of the nonprofit Everytown for Gun Safety. They reached out to students from other communities also affected by gun violence, especially students of color in urban areas, whose voices were often ignored. Leading by example, they mobilized young people throughout America to speak up for more gun control.

March organizers received an overwhelming show of support from around the country through social media posts and donations. Five short weeks later, the March for Our Lives was a reality. On March 24, 2018, more than 200,000 people of all ages and backgrounds met in Washington, DC, for the central march to protest the lack of gun control laws that left communities and schools vulnerable to gun violence, especially by assault rifles. Families, students, and supporters of those affected by gun violence crowded Pennsylvania Avenue, demanding that their lives and the safety of others become the priority, not guns, and calling for universal background checks and bans on assault-style weapons and high-capacity magazines (ammunition used in guns). They wanted lawmakers in Washington to know they were not going to back down and that many of them would soon have the power to vote. On each corner, volunteers in neon yellow encouraged people to register to vote. While politicians had told young people to stay silent and wait, by their numbers, they were saying they refused to do so. During the march, protesters took to social media, tweeting #MarchForOurLives nearly four million times. They believed gun violence could be fixed, and by marching, they wanted politicians to know they are the generation that is willing to fix it!

The March for Our Lives spawned nearly eight hundred "sibling marches" in the US and abroad and was one of the largest student-driven marches in history. Due in part to this youth-energized activism, in 2018 alone, sixty-seven gun safety bills in twenty-six states and DC were signed into law, and the number of youth voters rose by 31 percent, the highest turnout in years. But federal gun control has not yet been passed, so young people continue to come together to march and be voices for change, seeking to protect their lives, those of their neighbors and peers, and all of their futures from bullets and laws that do not adequately keep them safe.

#NEVER AGAIN

YOUTH CLIMATE STRIKE
"FRIDAYS FOR FUTURE"

Stockholm, Sweden, and Worldwide
March 15, 2019

People tell us that we can't change climate change because we're just kids . . . but we still have a voice. We still have the ability to stand up for something. We need to stand up for our right to protect our future. . . .

—Sabirah Mahmud, lead organizer of Philadelphia Youth Climate Strike

TOGETHER WE MARCH BECAUSE OUR PLANET, THIS GENERATION, AND FUTURE GENERATIONS ARE RUNNING OUT OF TIME

While in the US we have marched for stronger gun control and protections for undocumented minors, activists all over the world have been calling for *everyone* to focus on climate change. The earth's climate is altering rapidly, and this change has an effect on the air, land, and animals, and on each of us. As global temperatures increase, oceans grow warmer and expand, glaciers melt faster, and sea levels rise. This causes animals to migrate and attempt to adapt to more hostile environments, crops to die, and people's livelihoods and communities to be affected by droughts, wildfires, and heat waves. The elderly and the poor are especially vulnerable to these harsh elements.

For many years, scientists and climate activists around the world have issued warnings about the climate crisis, explaining that humans carry much of the blame for the increase because we add more greenhouse gases, such as carbon dioxide (CO_2), from man-made sources like power plants, electricity, cars, trucks, and planes into the atmosphere. Unfortunately, politicians and CEOs who could help reverse this impact have not listened. So, in August of 2018, a fifteen-year-old in Stockholm, Sweden, decided to act herself. She was in part inspired by Black civil rights activist Rosa Parks, an introvert like her, who had refused to leave her bus seat for a white person, igniting a bus boycott. Greta Thunberg now believed there was a way her voice could be heard too, so she took a seat on the sidewalk outside the Swedish parliament, refusing to go to school. She realized that by refusing to do something, just like Rosa Parks did, she could potentially make a difference too.

GRETA THUNBERG

Greta refused to attend classes until Swedish officials took a more proactive role in dealing with issues of the climate. Eventually more students joined her, as well as adults, including the media. Some stood in support, others told her to go back to school, but soon her supporters outnumbered her critics and it did not take long for her example to catch on.

Young people were inspired by someone their age taking a stand for their future, like the Parkland students did in America. Soon thousands of them started walking out of their classrooms each Friday, calling it Fridays for Future. Some protested for a few minutes, others for the full day. They understood each act of defiance was important. Greta told her peers that just like other youth-led movements, they needed to turn their anger into action and fight for their future since many adults did not seem to deem it a priority.

And that is exactly what over 1.4 million young activists across the globe did on March 15, 2019. They marched! When Greta called for a global youth climate strike, her peers around the world mobilized. Though they had no legal power, they understood they could not wait until they were older, because then it would be too late for their generation. Scientists said they had eleven more years until climate change became irreversible. So, at 11:00 a.m., to symbolize the eleven years, student-led and student-organized protests began. Instead of going to class, students marched. One group led with the banner, WE'RE MISSING OUR LESSONS SO WE CAN TEACH YOU ONE.

There were 2,052 reported events, in at least 123 countries. In Sydney, Australia, at least 30,000 marched from Town Hall Square to Hyde Park. In Delhi, India, 200 students marched out of their classrooms into the streets. In Tokyo, Japan, students marched from United Nations University through the capital in a busy shopping district. And in Kampala, Uganda, when the fourteen-year-old organizer was denied a permit to march along a busy downtown street with one hundred other grade school and university students, she simply used another street! Together, through the power of social media and through Greta's unwavering focus and example, marchers everywhere were energized and determined not to give up until the climate crisis became a priority for every lawmaker and world citizen.

The fight to address the climate crisis is far from over, but through the awareness that young voices like Greta's—and those of Autumn Peltier, Xiye Bastida, Isra Hirsi, and Amariyanna Copeny, to name a few—have brought to the cause, the climate is at the forefront of many conversations and policy discussions. In March 2019, Greta Thunberg, who once thought of herself as invisible, was nominated for the Nobel Peace Prize. One girl refusing to accept the status quo helped build and energize a whole movement that continues to march on today.

JUSTICE FOR GEORGE FLOYD
AND BLACK LIVES MATTER PROTESTS

Minneapolis, Minnesota; Nashville, Tennessee; and Worldwide
May 26, 2020, and beyond

what does unity look like? this is what unity looks like. change is coming. we see it we feel it, we know it. A new revolution is on the way.

—Teens4Equality Instagram post, June 5, 2020

TOGETHER WE MARCH DURING A PANDEMIC BECAUSE BLACK LIVES DO MATTER

Since the 2014 NAACP Youth March, names of victims such as Trayvon Martin, Kayla Moore, Walter Scott, Eric Garner, Tamir Rice, Natasha McKenna, Freddie Gray, Sandra Bland, Philando Castile, Stephon Clark, Atatiana Jefferson, Ahmaud Arbery, Breonna Taylor, and countless others joined Michael Brown's in news stories of police brutality and racism that got little attention outside their communities and always seemed to come to the same end—outrage from the Black community and headlines, but often few consequences or changes to stop such inexcusable tragedies from happening again. But then in May of 2020, a particular incident captured on video claimed the attention of the United States and many nations around the world. It was not the first time there was video evidence of police killing an unarmed Black person, but it had a much different effect for so many who saw it.

On May 25, 2020, George Floyd, a forty-six-year-old Black man, was arrested by police for allegedly paying a store clerk with a counterfeit twenty-dollar bill. Though there were many bystanders, it was the video footage recorded by a seventeen-year-old that would help create a multicultural movement. People around the world watched as her footage showed that for up to eight minutes and forty-six seconds, a white Minneapolis police officer pressed his knee onto the neck of a handcuffed George Floyd while two other officers restrained his chest and legs with their full weight, cutting off his ability to breathe, and another officer stood by and watched. Despite his cries of "I can't breathe" and urgent pleas for help, along with onlookers' calls to aid, not harm him, the officers did not move or let up, and Mr. Floyd was killed.

The video surfaced as the deep-rooted inequalities and racist slashes in the fabric of society in the United States were being highlighted. The world was trying to make sense of a highly infectious respiratory virus, COVID-19, that was killing hundreds of thousands of people worldwide. Black, brown, and Indigenous communities were affected in much higher numbers. This magnified long-standing health, economic, and social inequalities. Often these injustices went ignored or unnoticed by a number of Americans, especially white people; however, many could no longer ignore this stark imbalance. In a similar way, the video of the killing of George Floyd forced many in the country to face the fact that Black people were also under ongoing threat of death at the hands of police because of the color of their skin.

Instantly the world reacted like it never had before. Though largely ignited by disgust over the officers' apparent blatant and sustained disregard for Mr. Floyd's life and the unnecessary aggression used against a man who was handcuffed and compliant, millions were also deeply troubled by the other officers' inaction and seeming lack of concern for his repeated calls for help. For the first time, many witnessed firsthand what Black communities have been speaking out against since before the Civil Rights movement and Jim Crow: that some of those called to protect and serve create the violence that brutalizes Black lives. That race, as they were seeing in so many facets of life and in one appalling incident after another, *did* have a profound effect on quality of life.

Protesters began to organize, and soon the number of marches was in the hundreds and then the thousands. Marches were multigenerational and multiracial. Some were led by longtime activists and some by those new to speaking out. Many of those newfound leaders were young people. By June 4, 2020, ten days after George Floyd's death, fifteen-year-old Zee Thomas and five other Nashville teen girls between the ages of fourteen and sixteen (Nya Collins, Jade Fuller, Kennedy Green, Emma Rose Smith, and Mikayla Smith) had organized and started an Instagram page and a coalition called Teens4Equality. They were ready to lead Nashville in a march. With the help of the local Black Lives Matter Nashville chapter and other supporters who got the word out, they staged the largest protest in the region's history since the lunch counter sit-ins of the 1960s. Like in marches all across the world, people came to lend their hearts, their bodies, and their support to protect Black lives. More than 10,000 people marched for almost five hours advocating for policing reform. The young women who led the Nashville march wore T-shirts that read: THE REVOLUTION STARTS WITH US, WE NEED CHANGE, WHAT'S DONE IN THE DARK, M*E*L*A*N*I*N, and WE MAKE IT HAPPEN.

The death of George Floyd was the spark so many like them needed to no longer sit by in silence. People worldwide of different ethnic backgrounds gathered for weeks and weeks, shouting, "Black Lives Matter," "Black Trans Lives Matter," and "Black Kids Matter." Marches against police violence and for Black lives took place in all fifty states and the District of Columbia.

While this movement has had far more support than ever in the past, it's not been without resistance. Much attention was focused by some on looters and rioters, with the aim of detracting from the positive strides of the majority of peace-minded protesters and their agenda. But these racist tactics did not stop marchers seeking equality for all and the dismantling of the systemic and deeply embedded racism in everyday life and institutions like the police force. And while in the past these tragedies and ensuing protests often led to little real change, this time the world seems to be taking largely unified action and refusing to back down. Many lawmakers and police departments are listening and working with communities toward that change. Confederate flags and symbols have been removed by state governments and businesses. Companies that had long remained silent showed support of #BlackLivesMatter and began to look at their own role in the perpetuation of racism. And the movement has become not just a call against racism, but a call to be anti-racist— which involves an active effort to oppose and dismantle racism in all forms. But most of all, more people than ever from varied backgrounds and lived experiences demanded a collective change and refused to let up. There is still a long way to go in dismantling the system of racism, but these protests have encouraged many to act, and have shown that even long-obstructed change can start to happen when we all come together and march.

CONCLUSION

FROM MOTHER JONES TO GRETA THUNBERG TO THE TRAGIC DEATH OF GEORGE FLOYD, WE'VE SEEN HOW ALL IT TAKES IS ONE PERSON STANDING UP FOR SOMETHING OR AN UNJUST MOMENT CAPTURED FOR THE WORLD TO SEE TO INSPIRE THOUSANDS TO COME TOGETHER AND MAKE THE CHANGE THEY ARE SEEKING POSSIBLE. IN MARCHING TOGETHER, ALL OF US AS INDIVIDUALS NEED TO MAKE THE CHOICE NOT ONLY TO PROTECT THE RIGHTS OF OURSELVES AND OUR FAMILIES, BUT TO HOLD DEAR AND PROTECT THE RIGHTS OF OUR FELLOW CITIZENS AS WELL. TOGETHER WE MARCH FOR MANY THINGS — PROTECTION, EQUALITY, LEARNING, INDEPENDENCE, EXISTENCE, ACCEPTANCE, UNDERSTANDING, AND LIFE — BUT MOST OF ALL, WE MARCH FOR ONE ANOTHER, SO THAT ALL OF US MIGHT HAVE A BETTER LIFE IN THE WORLD WE SHARE.

AUTHOR'S NOTE

**That which is hateful to you
do not do to your neighbors.**

—Hillel the Elder

Living in DC, you see marches occurring frequently for almost every cause, but in 2017 I was fascinated by the wave of these protests unfolding across the country and the world. It felt like the world had been rattled awake. Soon, I started researching other moments in history, both large and small, when people were shaken enough to protest as we do now. I was immediately struck by some of the overlapping themes that continue today from as far back as the nineteenth century—fair pay, safety, fairness, freedom, survival, a voice, and a place to belong. People have marched over and over, sometimes at great risk to themselves, to force us as the public to think about unfair working conditions, war, education, racism, injustice, and a multitude of issues that affect so many. Sometimes the marches brought about enormous change, greater awareness, or started determined movements. Other times a march was simply a moment of togetherness, where a group of people collectively took a stand for what they believe. Where anger turned to motivation, then action. Where one courageous voice became many. Where someone stood taller, realizing they weren't alone in their beliefs. But no matter what, they all kept going. Often it was their signs that told the stories of their frustrations, their grievances, their hopes, and their demands. And as I looked through countless images, three signs from two different points in history stood out to me—young people fighting the same fights in different eras. Their signs spoke of GAY POWER, BLACK POWER, WOMEN POWER, STUDENT POWER. They said, IN MY HOUSE WE BELIEVE BLACK LIVES MATTER, WOMEN'S RIGHTS ARE HUMAN RIGHTS, NO HUMAN IS ILLEGAL, SCIENCE IS REAL, LOVE IS LOVE, KINDNESS IS EVERYTHING. As one little girl's sign in the 1970s reads: NONE OF US IS FREE, UNTIL ALL OF US ARE FREE, and for me, that can't be truer or more apparent than today. So I know these words will stay firmly in my heart and mind and that they will inspire me, and I hope all of us will join them in never stopping to march together until the world is truly free.

WE want time to play

JULY 7–29, 1903
MARCH OF THE MILL CHILDREN
PHILADELPHIA, PENNSYLVANIA, TO
OYSTER BAY, NEW YORK

BE RIGHT AND PERSIST

FEBRUARY 9, 1907
MUD MARCH
LONDON, ENGLAND

JULY 28, 1917
SILENT PROTEST PARADE
NEW YORK, NEW YORK

GIVE US A CHANCE TO LIV

SO TREAT US SO WE MAY LOVE OUR COUNTRY

MARCH 12 – APRIL 6, 1930
THE SALT MARCH
AHMEDABAD, INDIA,
TO DANDI, INDIA

MAY 24, 1943
BULGARIAN JEWS MARCH
SOFIA, BULGARIA

Jim Crow MUST GO

PURE MILK NOT POISON

MAY 2 – 7, 1963
THE CHILDREN'S MARCH
BIRMINGHAM, ALABAMA

NOVEMBER 1, 1961
WOMEN STRIKE FOR
PEACE
NATIONWIDE

LIVE & WORK TOGETHER

STAND FOR WHAT YOU BELIEVE

AUGUST 28, 1963
MARCH ON WASHINGTON
FOR JOBS AND FREEDOM
WASHINGTON, DC

NOVEMBER 20, 1964
FREE SPEECH MOVEMENT
AND MARCH
BERKELEY, CALIFORNIA

LARRY HITT

RICHARD McGuIRE

NGO DAI

Sơn Mỹ

MARCH 17 – APRIL 10, 1966
DELANO TO SACRAMENTO MARCH
DELANO, CALIFORNIA, TO
SACRAMENTO, CALIFORNIA

NOVEMBER 13 – 15, 1969
MORATORIUM TO END
THE WAR IN VIETNAM
WASHINGTON, DC

Stanley E. Brown

BÌNH HÒA

SEPTEMBER 13, 1989
CAPE TOWN PEACE MARCH
CAPE TOWN, SOUTH AFRICA

ACCESS IS A CIVIL RIGHT

MARCH 12, 1990
CAPITOL CRAWL
WASHINGTON, DC

CHILDREN TO SCHOOL
ADULTS TO WORK
EXPLOITERS TO JAIL

JANUARY 17 - JUNE 1, 1998
GLOBAL MARCH AGAINST CHILD LABOUR
MANILA, PHILIPPINES; GENEVA,
SWITZERLAND; AND WORLDWIDE

FEBRUARY 11 - JULY 15, 1978
THE LONGEST WALK
SAN FRANCISCO, CALIFORNIA,
TO WASHINGTON, DC

NOVEMBER 3, 2012
MILLION PUPPET MARCH
WASHINGTON, DC

JANUARY 22, 2013
WANYAMA URITHI WETU WALK
"WILDLIFE IS OUR HERITAGE WALK"
NAIROBI, KENYA

KNOW PUPPETS, KNOW PEACE

MAKE PUPPETS NOT WAR

keep your MITTS off PBS!!

SAY IT CLEAR
SAY IT LOUD
GAY IS GOOD AND
GAY IS PROUD!

JUNE 28, 1970
CHRISTOPHER STREET
LIBERATION DAY MARCH
NEW YORK, NEW YORK

BLACK LIVES MATTER

AUGUST 23, 2014
NAACP YOUTH MARCH
FERGUSON, MISSOURI

BUILD BRIDGES NOT WALLS

JANUARY 21, 2017
WOMEN'S MARCH
WASHINGTON, DC, AND
WORLDWIDE

APRIL 22, 1970
EARTH DAY MARCH
ALBUQUERQUE, NEW MEXICO,
AND NATIONWIDE

MARCH 15, 2019
YOUTH CLIMATE STRIKE
STOCKHOLM, SWEDEN, AND
WORLDWIDE

THERE IS NO PLANET B

MARCH 24, 2018
MARCH FOR OUR LIVES
WASHINGTON, DC,
AND WORLDWIDE

**FEBRUARY 15 -
MARCH 1, 2018**
THE WALK TO STAY HOME
NEW YORK, NEW YORK,
TO WASHINGTON, DC

Silence is VIOLENCE #BLM

RACISM IS THE REAL VIRUS

stop killing us

BLACK LI

MAY 26, 2020, AND BEYOND
JUSTICE FOR GEORGE AND
BLACK LIVES MATTER PROTESTS
MINNEAPOLIS, MINNESOTA;
NASHVILLE, TENNESSEE; AND
WORLDWIDE

SELECTED BIBLIOGRAPHY

For a full bibliography, visit leahhendersonbooks.com/my-writing/picture-books/work-cited-further-reading-together-we-march/.

"There's something about a march . . ." Levy, Jacques E. *Cesar Chavez: Autobiography of La Causa*. Minneapolis: University of Minnesota Press, 2007, p. 210.

MARCH OF THE MILL CHILDREN

"Sometimes it takes . . ." "Across the Delaware." *The Courier-News*, July 11, 1903, p. 3.

". . . the most dangerous women . . ." Gorn, Elliott J. *Mother Jones: The Most Dangerous Woman in America*. New York: Hill and Wang, 2002, pp. 96–97; Atkinson, Linda. *Mother Jones, the Most Dangerous Woman in America*. New York: Crown Publishers, 1978; Jones, Mary Harris. The Autobiography of Mother Jones. New York: Prism Key Press, 2011.

MUD MARCH

"Rise Up, Women . . ." Mills, Theodora. "Rise Up Women!" The Suffragists. http://www.thesuffragettes.org/resources/anthems/; Fawcett, Millicent Garrett. *What I Remember*. New York: G. P. Putnam's Sons, 1925; Frye, Kate P. *Campaigning for the Vote: Kate Parry Frye's Suffrage Diary*, edited by Elizabeth Crawford. London: Francis Boutle Publishers, 2013.

THE SILENT PROTEST PARADE

"We live in spite of death shadowing us . . ." NAACP. Flyer distributed before the Negro Silent Protest Parade, New York, July 28, 1917. https://nationalhumanitiescenter.org/pds/maai2/forward/text4/silentprotest.pdf; "The Negro Silent Parade." *The Crisis* 14 no. 5 (September 1917): 241–244 ; "Negroes in Protest March in Fifth Av." *New York Times*, July 29, 1917, p. 12.

THE SALT MARCH

"I want world sympathy . . ." Gandhi, Mahatma. "Gandhi's Salt March, the Nonviolent Journey That Changed the World." *MSNBC*. http://www.msnbc.com/msnbc/inside-gandhis-salt-march-the-nonviolent-journey-changed-the-world#slide11; Weber, Thomas. *On the Salt March: The Historiography of Gandhi's March to Dandi*. New Delhi: Rupa & Co, 2009; Associated Press. "Gandhi Makes Salt, Defying India's Law." *New York Times*, April 6, 1930.

BULGARIAN JEWS MARCH

"You know what you have to do . . ." Bar-Zohar, Michael. *Beyond Hitler's Grasp: The Heroic Rescue of Bulgaria's Jews*. Avon, MA: Adams Media Corporation, 2001, p. 193; Gelber, N. M. "Jewish Life in Bulgaria." *Jewish Social Studies* 8, no. 2 (April 1946): 103–126. *Empty Boxcars: Bulgaria's Jews Deportation and Holocaust*. Directed by Ed Gaffney. New York: Gamut Media, 2011.

WOMEN STRIKE FOR PEACE

"The sit-in strikers have reminded us . . ." Associated Press. "Thousands of Women Join in Plea for Peace." *Los Angeles Times*, November 2, 1961; Swerdlow, Amy. *Women Strike for Peace*, Chicago: University of Chicago Press, 1993; "The First Strike: November 1, 1961," The History of Women Strike for Peace. https://womenstrikeforpeace.com/history/the-first-strike-november-1-1961/.

THE CHILDREN'S MARCH

"Don't worry about your children . . ." King, Martin Luther Jr. Opening address delivered at Birmingham mass meeting May 6, 1963. Folkways Records Collection, Smithsonian Institution, Center for Folklife Programs and Cultural Studies, Washington, DC; King, Martin Luther Jr. "Freedom Now!" *The Autobiography of Martin Luther King Jr.*, edited by Clayborne Carson, p. 205-217. New York: Grand Central Publishing, 1998. McWhorter, Diane. *Carry Me Home: Birmingham, Alabama, the Climactic Battle of the Civil Rights Revolution*. New York: Simon & Schuster, 2001.

MARCH ON WASHINGTON FOR JOBS AND FREEDOM

"We must say: 'Wake up America!'" Lewis, John. "We Must Say: Wake Up America!" Speech at March on Washington, Washington, DC, August 28, 1963. Voices of Democracy: The U.S. Oratory Project. https://voicesofdemocracy.umd.edu/lewis-speech-at-the-march-on-washington-speech-text/; Educational Radio Network. "March on Washington for Jobs and Freedom," parts 1–17," August 18, 1963. WGBH Media Library & Archives. http://openvault.wgbh.org/collections/march_on_washington/ern-coverage; Fletcher, Michael, and Ryan R. Reed. "An Oral History of the March on Washington." *Smithsonian Magazine*, July 2013. Video, https://www.smithsonianmag.com/history/oral-history-march-washington-180953863/.

FREE SPEECH MOVEMENT AND MARCH

"There's a time . . ." Savio, Mario. "Operation of the Machine." Speech at Sproul Hall Sit-in, Berkeley, California, December 2, 1964. https://youtu.be/lsO_SIA7E8k.

". . . not an end . . ." King, Martin Luther Jr. "I Have a Dream." Speech, Washington, DC, August 28, 1962. The Martin Luther King Jr. Research and Education Institute. https://kinginstitute.stanford.edu/king-papers/documents/i-have-dream-address-delivered-march-washington-jobs-and-freedom; Lunsford, Terry F. "The Berkeley Student Protests, 1964–65" in the "Free Speech Crises at Berkeley, 1964–1965," December 1965. Online Archive California. https://oac.cdlib.org/view?docId=kt9r29p975;NAAN=13030&doc.view=frames&chunk.id=div00002&toc.depth=1&toc.id=&brand=oac4; Free Speech Movement Archives. http://www.fsm-a.org/

DELANO TO SACRAMENTO MARCH

"I feel we have the same rights as any of them . . ." Guillermo, Emil. "Restoring Larry Itliong to His Rightful Place During Filipino American History Month." Asian American Legal Defense and Education Fund, October 16, 2013. https://www.aaldef.org/blog/restoring-larry-itliong-to-his-rightful-place-during-filipino-american-history-month/; Levy, Jacques E. *Cesar Chavez: Autobiography of La Causa.* Minneapolis: University of Minnesota Press, 2007; *ViewFinder.* Season 19, episode 6, "Delano Manongs. Directed by Marissa Aroy. PBS, aired May 06, 2014. https://www.pbs.org/video/kvie-viewfinder-delano-manongs/.

MORATORIUM TO END THE WAR IN VIETNAM

"Nothing is more precious . . ." Fuchs-Abrams, Sabrina. "Women on War: Mary McCarthy, Susan Sontag, and Diana Trilling Debate the Vietnam War." *Women's Studies* 37: 8 (November 2008) 987–1007, https://doi.org/10.1080/00497870802414496; Herbers, Joan. "250,000 War Protesters Stage a Peaceful March and Rally in Heart of Washington." *New York Times,* November 16, 1969; Lunch, William L., and Peter W. Sperlich. "American Public Opinion and the War in Vietnam." *Western Political Quarterly* 32, No. 1 (March 1979): 21–44. https://www.jstor.org/stable/447561?read-now=1&seq=5#metadata_info_tab_contents.

EARTH DAY MARCH

"We are going to make people understand . . ." Sandoval, Arturo. *CBS News with Walter Cronkite.* April 22, 1970. https://www.youtube.com/watch?v=UwGGMwpt2HU.

"Each year, new species of animals are added . . ." United States Congress. *Congressional Record* 115, part 2. US Government Printing Office, October 8, 1969, p. 1268. https://play.google.com/books/reader?id=F53AaZuVEq0C&hl=en&pg=GBS.PA29126; Nelson Institute for Environmental Studies. "A Proposal Reprinted Across the Country." *Gaylord Nelson and Earth Day.* http://www.nelsonearthday.net/earth-day/proposal.php; Earth Day Network. "The History of Earth Day." https://www.earthday.org/about/the-history-of-earth-day/.

THE CHRISTOPHER STREET LIBERATION DAY MARCH

"Now we've walked . . ." Franke-Ruta, Garance. "An Amazing 1969 Account of the Stonewall Uprising." *The Atlantic.* January 24, 2013. https://www.theatlantic.com/politics/archive/2013/01/an-amazing-1969-account-of-the-stonewall-uprising/272467/.

"If you are gay . . ." Farber, Jim. "Before the Stonewall Uprising, There Was the 'Sip-In'," *New York Times,* April 20, 2016; Garcia, Michelle. "From Our Archives: The 1969 *Advocate* Article on the Stonewall Riots." *Advocate,* June 29, 2012. https://www.advocate.com/society/activism/2012/06/29/our-archives-1969-advocate-article-stonewall-riots; Sargeant, Fred. "1970: A First-Person Account of the First Gay Pride March." Villagevoice.com. June 22, 2010. https://www.villagevoice.com/2010/06/22/1970-a-first-person-account-of-the-first-gay-pride-march/.

THE LONGEST WALK

". . . on this walk I learned . . ." Ranck, Lee. "To Save Their Indian Way of Life." *Engage/Social Action* 6, no. 41 (September 1978); 4–7; "Over 5,000 End Longest Walk." *Off Our Backs* 8, no. 5 (Aug–Sept 1978): 4; Valentine, Paul W., and Patricia Camp. "Indians March Into Capital." *Washington Post,* July 16, 1978. https://www.washingtonpost.com/archive/politics/1978/07/16/indians-march-into-capital/9be45792-bf44-402c-afae-5b34ae1e8b10/?utm_term=.ca7e50510b67.

CAPE TOWN PEACE MARCH

"Nothing, nothing . . ." "Message from Patron Archbishop Emeritus Desmond Tutu," Glimpsing Hope, Marching for Peace: A Commemoration of the 13 September 1989 Cape Town Peace March

"We are going to defy . . ." "Tutus, 34 marchers arrested." *Berkshire Eagle,* September 2, 1989; *Glimpsing Hope, Marching For Peace: A Commemoration of the 13 September 1989 Cape Town Peace March.* St. Georges Cathedral Crypt Memory and Witness Centre, 2009; Kraft, Scott. "Tutu Leads 20,000 in Peaceful S. Africa March; No Police Intervention." *Los Angeles Times,* September 14, 1989. http://articles.latimes.com/1989-09-14/news/mn-275_1_south-africa.

CAPITOL CRAWL

"The greatest lesson of the civil rights movement . . ." Aquino, Jay, and TJ Hill, eds. "Speaking for Yourself: The Ed Roberts Story." *DCRC Voice,* January 2019. https://www.dcrc.co/wp-content/uploads/2019/01/Voice-the-DCRC-Newsletter-January-2019.pdf.

"I'll take all night if I have to . . ." Welch, William M. "Disabled Climb Capitol Steps to Plea for Government Protection." *AP News,* March 12, 1990. https://apnews.com/2672c50ca9c6155ed0cc3a4e36bdc20c.

"Let the shameful wall . . ." US National Archives. "President George H. W. Bush Signs the Americans with Disabilities Act, 07/26/1990." YouTube video, 22:36. July 15, 2015. https://youtu.be/-cNcE48Xjw8; Burgdorf Jr., Robert L. "Why I Wrote the Americans with Disabilities Act." *Washington Post,* July 24, 2015. https://www.washingtonpost.com/posteverything/wp/2015/07/24/why-the-americans-with-disabilities-act-mattered/; Switzer, Jacqueline V. *Disabled Rights: American Disability Policy and the Fight for Equality.* Washington, DC: Georgetown University Press, 2003.

GLOBAL MARCH AGAINST CHILD LABOR

"My whole life has just one single aim . . ." Satyarthi, Kailash. Speech. Nobel Peace Prize Concert, December 11, 2014. YouTube video, 8:36. October 12, 2015. https://www.youtube.com/watch?v=9AJfv5pgxZE.

"Worst Forms of Child Labour . . ." "The Worst Forms of Child Labour," International Labour Organization. http://www.ilo.org/ipec/Campaignandadvocacy/Youthinaction/C182-Youth-orientated/worstforms/lang--en/index.htm; Global March Website. https://globalmarch.org; "Global March Against Child Labor Arrives in the United States." *International Labor Rights Forum.* May 1, 1998. https://laborrights.org/in-the-news/global-march-against-child-labor-arrives-united-states.

MILLION MUPPET MARCH

"This is all about . . ." MillionPuppets. "Million Puppet March Documentary—2012." YouTube video, 14:20. January 15, 2018. https://www.youtube.com/watch?v=zeA0uc8FdGY.

"America's largest classroom . . ." "Alternative Sources of Funding for Public Broadcasting Stations." Washington, DC: Corporation for Public Broadcasting, June 20, 2012, p. 7.

" . . . best fuzzy, feathered, felted friends . . ." Million Puppet March Website, October 4, 2012. https://millionpuppetmarch.com/page/8; Million Muppet March. "About the Organizers." Millionpuppetmarch.com. Accessed 5/12/19. https://millionpuppetmarch.com/about-us; Judkis, Maura. "The Million Puppet March: Fighting for Public Broadcasting with Felt and Fur." *Washington Post*, November 3, 2012; Overbey, Erin. "Mitt Romney, Big Bird, and the Million Puppet March." *New Yorker*, November 2, 2012. https://www.newyorker.com/books/double-take/mitt-romney-big-bird-and-the-million-puppet-march; Samakow, Jessica. "Million Puppet March Takes Washington: Families Rally in Support of Public TV and Radio." *HuffPost*, November 5, 2012.

WANYAMA URITHI WETU WALK

"We don't want to wait . . ." "Thousands March Worldwide for Rhino, Elephant Protection." *Straits Times*, October 5, 2014. https://www.straitstimes.com/world/africa/thousands-march-worldwide-for-rhino-elephant-protection; KUAPO. "Nairobi Wanyama Urithi Wetu Walk: 22.01.2013." YouTube video, 11:28. March 12, 2013. https://www.youtube.com/watch?v=A8GTjr86tW8; Warner, Gregory. "African Leaders: No One Country Can Stop Elephant Poaching." *Morning Edition.* National Public Radio, Washington, DC, NPR, August 5, 2014. https://www.npr.org/sections/parallels/2014/08/05/337973375/african-countries-say-they-need-help-to-stop-elephant-poaching.

NAACP YOUTH MARCH

"It means a lot to me . . ." Chappell, Bill. "Mo. Highway Patrol Takes Over Security in Ferguson, Governor Says." *The Two-Way.* National Public Radio, Washington, DC, NPR, August 14, 2014. https://www.npr.org/sections/thetwo-way/2014/08/14/340315497/tear-gas-and-arrests-ferguson-police-and-protesters-face-off.

"I continue to be surprised . . ." Sanders, Joshunda. "Five Years In, Hearing the Voices of Black Lives Matter." *Village Voice*, July 30, 2018. https://www.npr.org/sections/thetwo-way/2014/08/14/340315497/tear-gas-and-arrests-ferguson-police-and-protesters-face-off.

"We have to kind of refocus . . ." Not in Our Town. "Community Gathers at NAACP Youth March for Michael Brown (Ferguson Conversations)." YouTube video, 2:39. October 9, 2014. https://www.youtube.com/watch?time_continue=2&v=ffXW5fPJVvQ&feature=emb_logo; Buchanan, Larry, Ford Fessenden, K. K. Rebecca Lai, Haeyoun Park, Alicia Parlapiano, Archie Tse, Tim Wallace, Derek Watkins, and Karen Yourish. "Q & A: What Happened in Ferguson?" *New York Times*, August 10, 2014. https://www.nytimes.com/interactive/2014/08/13/us/ferguson-missouri-town-under-siege-after-police-shooting.html; Altman, Maria, and Camille Phillips. "Two Weeks After Brown Died: NAACP Youth March." St. Louis Public Radio, August 24, 2014. https://news.stlpublicradio.org/post/two-weeks-after-brown-died-naacp-youth-march-stl-unity-rally-pro-wilson-group-raises-money#stream/0.

WOMEN'S MARCH

"We join in diversity . . ." Women's March on Washington. "Mission & Vision." Last modified 2017. https://web.archive.org/web/20170123015852/https://www.womensmarch.com/mission/

"Remember the ladies . . ." Allen, Erin. 2016. "Remember the Ladies." *Library of Congress* (blog), March 31, 2016. https://blogs.loc.gov/loc/2016/03/remember-the-ladies/.

"I think we should march . . ." Kearney, Laila. "Hawaii Grandma's Plea Launches Women's March in Washington." *Reuters*, December 5, 2016. https://www.reuters.com/article/us-usa-trump-women/hawaii-grandmas-plea-launches-womens-march-in-washington-idUSKBN13U0GW; Tolentino, Jia. "The Somehow Controversial Women's March on Washington." *The New Yorker*, January 18, 2017. https://www.newyorker.com/culture/jia-tolentino/the-somehow-controversial-womens-march-on-washington; Women's March on Washington. "About Us: Unity Principles." Last accessed 2/19/20. Women's March Website (archive). https://web.archive.org/web/20170122172427/https://static1.squarespace.com/static/584086c7be6594762f5ec56e/t/587ffb20579fb3554668c111/1484782369253/WMW+Guiding+Vision+%26+Definition+of+Principles.pdf; Women's March on Washington. "On January 21, 2017, We Made History . . ." Last accessed 2/18/20. Women's March website (archive). https://web.archive.org/web/20170122173911/https://www.womensmarch.com/sister-stream/.

THE WALK TO STAY HOME

"It is time for us . . ." The Seed Project staff. "Immigrant Youth Launch Walk to Stay Home From New York to D.C." *PopularResistance.org*, February 19, 2018. https://popularresistance.org/immigrant-youth-launch-walk-to-stay-home-from-new-york-to-d-c/.

"We walk in community . . ." Cain, Rachel. "Activists Trek 250 Miles, Through the County on a Mission." *The Sentinel*, March 7, 2018.

https://pgs.thesentinel.com/2018/03/07/activists-trek-250-miles-through-the-county-on-a-mission/.

"I went down to the capital . . ." Movimiento Cosecha–The Seed Project. "Day 14 We Made It to Washington, DC. We Holding a Press Conference." Facebook Live video, 7:43. February 28, 2018. https://www.facebook.com/seedproject/videos/1786232718345498/.

"We will take a chance . . ." Alvarado, Monsy. "'Dreamers' Hope to Gain Support for Immigration Legislation on 250-Mile N.Y. to D.C. Walk." *North Jersey*, February 15, 2018. https://www.northjersey.com/story/news/nation/2018/02/15/dreamers-hope-gain-support-immigration-legislation-250-mile-n-y-d-c-walk/333636002/; Seed Project. "The Walk to Stay Home: A Journey of Hope." *The Action Network*. https://actionnetwork.org/forms/the-big-walk; "Movimiento Cosecha–The Seed Project." Facebook. https://www.facebook.com/seedproject/; Venugopal, Arun. "An Immigrant Trek, From NYC to DC." *WNYC News*, February 15, 2018. https://www.wnyc.org/story/immigrant-trek-nyc-dc/.

MARCH FOR OUR LIVES

"We are the turn of this century . . ." Middleton, Mya. "Mya Middleton Speaks at March for Our Lives—'We Deserve Better.'" Speech, March for Our Lives. YouTube video, 4:21. March 24, 2018. https://www.youtube.com/watch?v=MrQvbEX1ylQ; March for Our Lives. "Mission Statement." March for Our Lives Website. https://marchforourlives.com/mission-statement/; Grinberg, Emanuella, and Nadeem Muaddi. "How the Parkland Students Pulled Off a Massive National Protest in Only 5 Weeks." *CNN*, March 26, 2018. https://www.cnn.com/2018/03/26/us/march-for-our-lives/index.html.

YOUTH CLIMATE STRIKE

"People tell us . . ." Ramirez, Rachel. "Students Share Motivations Ahead of Youth Climate Strike. *Grist*, March 14, 2019. https://grist.org/article/students-share-motivations-ahead-of-youth-climate-strike/; Aronoff, Kate. "How Greta Thunberg's Lone Strike Against Climate Change Became a Global Movement." *Rolling Stone*, March 5, 2019. https://www.rollingstone.com/politics/politics-features/greta-thunberg-fridays-for-future-climate-change-800675/?jwsource=cl; Thunberg, Greta, Anna Taylor, and others. "Think We Should Be at School? Today's Climate Strike Is the Biggest Lesson of All." *The Guardian*, March 15, 2019. https://www.theguardian.com/commentisfree/2019/mar/15/school-climate-strike-greta-thunberg.

JUSTICE FOR GEORGE FLOYD AND BLACK LIVES MATTER PROTESTS

"what does unity look like?" Teens4Equality. 2020. "this is amazing. It's inspiring . . ." Instagram photo, June 5, 2020 posted. Accessed 6/24/20. https://www.instagram.com/p/CBCgnD3BD71/?utm_source=ig_embed.

Elizabeth, De. "Teen Activists Organized a Massive Black Lives Matter Protest in Nashville." *Teen Vogue*, June 7, 2020. Online. https://www.teenvogue.com/story/teenage-activists-black-lives-matter-protest-nashville.

Bosman, Julie, and Amy Harmon. "Protests Draw Shoulder-to-Shoulder Crowds After Months of Virus Isolation." *The New York Times*. June 2, 2020. Online. https://www.nytimes.com/2020/06/02/us/coronavirus-protests-george-floyd.html.

Fox, Maggie. "Demonstrators say it's worth braving coronavirus to protest George Floyd's killing." CNN, June 6, 2020. Online. https://www.cnn.com/2020/06/06/health/pandemic-protesters-covid-risk-floyd-trnd/index.html.

GENERAL BOOKS ABOUT ACTIVISM

Bland, Robert L., and Lynda B. Lowery. *The Little Book of Little Activists*. New York: Viking Books for Young Readers, 2017.

Braun, Eric. *Taking Action for Civil and Political Rights*. Minneapolis: Lerner Publications, 2017.

Freedman, Russell. *Because They Marched: The People's Campaign for Voting Rights That Changed America*. New York: Holiday House, 2014.

Halpin, Mikki. *It's Your World—If You Don't Like It, Change It: Activism for Teenagers*. New York: Simon Pulse, 2004.

Markel, Michelle, Melissa Sweet, and Rachel Zegar. *Brave Girl: Clara and the Shirtwaist Makers' Strike of 1909*. New York: Balzer + Bray, 2013.